SURVIVAL
AMAZING WILD ANIMALS
IN THE NATURAL WORLD

SURVIVAL
AMAZING WILD ANIMALS
IN THE NATURAL WORLD

MICHAEL CHINERY

LORENZ BOOKS

Contents

Animal Planet

As far as we know our planet is unique in the universe. It is the only one that is known to have life on it, and there is an extraordinary diversity of life forms. Scientists believe there could be between 14 and 100 million species of animals and plants living today. They cannot be sure exactly how many because most of them are too small to find or are living in unexplored places like the tropical rainforest or the deep sea. Of all those species only 1.3 million have been studied scientifically,

Lions must hunt down and kill their own food. They do this in groups, enabling them to bring down prey far bigger than themselves.

including about three-quarters of a million insects and fifty thousand vertebrates (animals with backbones), so there is still a great deal for us to learn. About 10,000 species are described annually, so it could possibly take up to 500 years to complete a catalogue of the earth's living creatures.

Inside the body of animals

Some of what we do know about is laid out in the pages of this book. We find out how every creature is adapted to the habitat in which it lives. Whether this is on land or in the sea, its ability

Wolves are very agile animals and this helps them to escape from predators; they can leap upwards, sideways and even backwards.

to survive depends not only on its size or shape, but also by what goes on inside its body. 'How Animals Work' peels away the layers to reveal the complex inner workings of all kinds of animals, and how they live in such a variety of different ways. It shows how almost every animal on the planet depends on plants for food and energy, whether it eats vegetation directly (a herbivore or plant-eater, such as horses, elephants and many insects) or hunts and kills animals that consume plants (a carnivore or meat-eater, such as lions, crocodiles and tigers). All have the means to gather or catch their chosen food and then process it and turn it into valuable energy.

Mother Nature and evolution

Animals need to be able to find their way about, locate food and detect the predators that are out to hunt them down. They must be able to move from one place to another to be in the best spot to maximize their chances of eating, to escape from predators, and also to track down a mate so that they can reproduce. 'Animal Survival' explores the senses of sight, smell, hearing, and touch, and discovers other senses that humans do not have and do not even understand. It reveals how animals have taken up every means to travel on land, under the sea and in the air, and it tells how Mother Nature adopted the same solution to the same challenge in different groups of animals that evolved many millions of years apart.

The owl is built to fly silently and to locate prey that it cannot see but can hear, so it can hunt in the dark.

Amazing animals

Some animals go to extraordinary lengths to survive in an often hostile world. Much like their human military equivalents animals indulge in chemical warfare, both for attack and defence. There are 'stealth' animals that use camouflage to make themselves invisible, while 'advertisers' have gaudy patterns to startle and frighten. In 'Amazing Animals', we find animals really are 'amazing', and none more so than those that travel enormous distances across the world, relying on the sun, stars and the earth's magnetic field to find their way across featureless oceans and deserts. Migratory animals escape extremes in the weather, but others opt out and hibernate when times are hard, and some keep going in all seasons, even in the harshest of places, like hot deserts, the ocean's abyss and the icy Arctic wilderness.

The threat of extinction

Wherever they are and whatever they do to survive, nothing prepared animals for the activities of people. In the short space of time that modern man has evolved – about 2 million years – animals have been disappearing more rapidly than before, and that decline is accelerating. Of the 1.7 million known species between five and twenty per cent are threatened with extinction. Half of them live in the tropical rainforests, and 50–100 species are disappearing every day. The blame for their downfall lies squarely on the shoulders of humankind. 'Animals in Danger' shows that unless there is a change in our attitude to the natural world, many species face a bleak future.

What the future holds

'Animal Planet' shows us an incredible global collection of animals. Finding out about the remarkable ways in which all these creatures live and work is perhaps the first step in understanding how they might be saved.

There are 17,500 known species of butterfly in the world. Of these about 300 are endangered.

7

How Animals Work

Inside every animal is an extraordinary story waiting to be told. This section provides an insight into how all kinds of animals feed, hunt and survive — examining the different physical characteristics that allow them to live in wild and dangerous conditions.

How Animals Work

Over a million different kinds or species of animals inhabit the Earth. They live on land and in the water and exhibit an amazing range of shapes and sizes, but they all have a number of things in common. They all move, feed, breathe, reproduce, grow and get rid of waste. These features are characteristic of all living things, but the animals' bodies are constructed to carry them out in many different ways. You will discover how various animals live, and how their bodies are made to do the jobs necessary to keep them fit and healthy.

Polar bears can swim in the icy sea because they are protected by insulating fur and layers of thick fat.

Muscles for Movement

Animals can run, hop, crawl, fly or swim, and these movements are all brought about by muscles. Each end of a muscle is firmly fixed to a part of the body and, when the muscle contracts, it makes something move. Among the vertebrates (animals with backbones) — most of the muscles

The muscles in the neck, shoulders and hindquarters of wolves are very well developed. They give the wolf strength, stamina and speed.

are attached to bones. Contraction of the muscles at the top of a wolf's leg, for example, pulls on the bones lower down in the leg and lifts the leg up. Other muscles swing it forward and put it down again — the faster this happens, the faster the wolf runs. All vertebrates are built on a similar plan, but the shape, arrangement and density of their bones vary. The skeleton of a bird's wing, for example, has the same basic structure as that of an ape's arm, but birds' bones, unlike mammals, are usually hollow. This makes them lighter, so flying is easier.

Invertebrate animals do not have bony skeletons, they have tough and sometimes very hard shells or cases (exoskeletons). Insects and spiders have lots of joints, rather like suits of armour. The joints are moved when they are pulled by muscles fixed to the insides of the armour.

Feeding

Food provides animals with energy and the materials needed
for growth. Digestive juices break it down into simple substances
that are absorbed into the body. Most animals specialize in either
liquid or solid food.

Bugs and butterflies feed on liquids, such as plant sap and
nectar, which they suck up through slender tubes. The drinking
tubes of bugs have sharp tips that pierce the plants to reach the
sap. Spiders feed on insects and other small animals, but they cannot
eat solid matter, so they liquefy their prey with digestive juices before
they swallow it. Beetles and many other insects have biting jaws and
eat solid food, but their jaws are outside their mouths and they chew
their food before pushing it into their mouths.

Most vertebrates have strong teeth, the shape and arrangement of
which depend on the kind of food that is eaten. Cats and other carnivorous
animals (meat-eaters) have sharp-edged teeth that slice through the meat.
Baleen whales have no teeth: they filter small creatures from the water with
the horny plates that hang from the roof of the mouth like curtains. Birds
also lack teeth. Their horny beaks do the same job as teeth and, being
lighter, they make it easier for the birds to fly.

*Insects are protected
by a hard outer layer
called an exoskeleton
which is waterproof
and also prevents the
insect from drying
out in hot weather.*

Breathing

Oxygen is necessary for life, and animals get oxygen from the air or water around them.
Vertebrates that live on the land breathe with lungs. Air is drawn into these thin-walled pouches
and the oxygen passes through the lung walls and into the blood vessels to be carried around the
body. Fish breathe with gills. These are
clusters of tiny thin-walled fingers in the
throat section. Water is taken in through
the mouth and pumped over the gills,
where the oxygen dissolved in it passes
into the blood. The water then passes out
through the gill slits. These slits are
easily seen in sharks, but in most fish
they are covered with a flap called an
operculum. Insects' bodies have a
number of tiny holes on each side.
These holes are called spiracles and are
easily seen in large caterpillars. They
lead into a network of minute tubes,
called tracheae, that carry air to all
parts of the insect's body.

*The cheetah is the world's fastest land animal and is fine-tuned
for speed. It has wide nostrils to breathe in as much oxygen as
possible and has specially adapted paws for running fast.*

Nature's Success Story

People like to think
that humans dominate Earth,
but insects could in many ways be
seen as far more successful. There
are over one million species (kinds)
of insects, and because they breed
very quickly they can adapt to all
kinds of conditions and can live
just about anywhere.

Scientists divide insects into groups
called orders. The insects in each
order share certain features. Beetles
and bugs are two of the largest insect
orders. The main difference between
them is that beetles have biting jaws
and bugs have sucking mouthparts.
So far, 350,000 different kinds of
beetles and 80,000 different kinds of
bugs have been found, but there are
probably many more species.

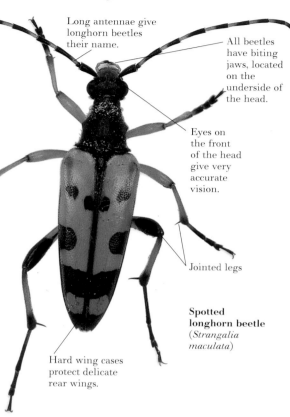

Long antennae give
longhorn beetles
their name.

All beetles
have biting
jaws, located
on the
underside of
the head.

Eyes on
the front
of the head
give very
accurate
vision.

Jointed legs

**Spotted
longhorn beetle**
(*Strangalia
maculata*)

Hard wing cases
protect delicate
rear wings.

▲ THE BEETLE ORDER
Beetles belong to the order Coleoptera, which
means 'sheath wings'. Most beetles have two
pairs of wings. The tough front wings fold over
the delicate rear wings to form a hard,
protective case, like body armour. Longhorn
beetles owe their name to their long antennae
(feelers), which look like long horns.

◄ LIVING IN WATER
Not all beetles and bugs live on land. Some,
like this great diving beetle, live in fresh water
ponds. The diving beetle hunts underwater,
diving down to catch a variety of small creatures.

◄ FEEDING TOGETHER

A group of aphids feeds on a plant stem, sucking up liquid sap. Most beetles and bugs live alone, but a few species, such as aphids, gather together in large numbers. Some insects, such as ants and bees, form communities. Living in a group gives them protection from predators.

What's in a Name?

This image comes from the animated feature film A Bug's Life. *The hero of the cartoon is not actually a bug at all, but an ant. True bugs are a particular group of insects with sucking mouthparts that can slurp up liquid food.*

Forest shield bug
(*Pentatoma rufipes*)

Six legs keep the bug stable as it scurries along the ground.

Antennae for touching and smelling

Thin wing-tip

Hard wing base

Tube-like mouthparts under the insect's head

Eyes on the sides of the head

◄ THE BUG ORDER

Bugs come in many shapes and sizes. All have long, jointed mouthparts that form a tube through which they suck up liquid food, like a syringe. Their order name is Hemiptera, which means 'half-wings'. The name refers to the front wings of many bugs, such as shield bugs, which are hard at the base and flimsy at the tip. With their wings folded, shield bugs are shaped like a warrior's shield.

THE YOUNG ONES ►

Many young insects, called larvae, look very different from the adults. This beetle larva, or grub, feeds on plant roots in the soil. Soon it will change into a winged adult. Young bugs, called nymphs, look like miniature adults when they hatch from their eggs although they have no wings.

Did you know? Insects are unique in having six legs – three on each side.

Bodies in Sections

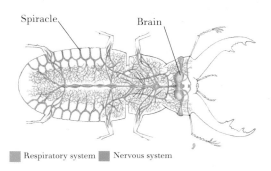

Garden chafer (*Phyllopertha horticola*)

Head

Thorax

Abdomen

Human bodies are supported on the inside by a bony skeleton. Insects do not have bones to support them but have a tough outer layer called an exoskeleton. This layer protects the insect's body from damage. The exoskeleton is also waterproof and helps to prevent the insect from drying out in hot weather. Holes in the exoskeleton, called spiracles, allow the insect to breathe.

The word 'insect' comes from the Latin word *insectum* meaning 'in sections'. All insect bodies are made up of three main parts. They have a head, a thorax (middle section) and an abdomen (rear section). Most adult insects have one or two pairs of wings. Many of them use long antennae to sense their surroundings.

▲ THREE SECTIONS

This beetle's main sense organs, the antennae and eyes, are on its head. Its wings and legs are attached to the thorax. The abdomen contains the most of the digestive and reproductive organs.

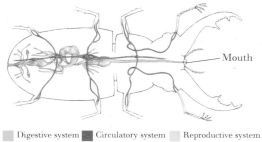

Spiracle

Brain

Mouth

■ Respiratory system ■ Nervous system

■ Digestive system ■ Circulatory system ■ Reproductive system

▲ BREATHING AND NERVOUS SYSTEMS

The respiratory (breathing) system has spiracles (holes) that lead to a network of tubes. The tubes allow air to reach all parts of the insect's body. The nervous system receives messages from the sense organs, and sends signals to the insect's muscles to make it move.

▲ OTHER BODY SYSTEMS

The digestive system breaks down food and absorbs it. The circulatory system includes a long, thin heart that pumps blood through the body. The abdomen contains the reproductive parts. Males have two testes that produce sperm. Females have two ovaries that produce eggs.

◀ IN COLD BLOOD

All insects, including beetles and bugs, are cold-blooded animals. This means that the temperature of their body is similar to their surroundings. Insects control their body temperature by moving about. To warm up, many insects bask in the sun, as this leaf beetle is doing. If they need to cool their bodies, they move into the shade.

SURVIVING THE COLD ▶

This tiger-beetle egg is buried in the soil. In some parts of the world, winters are too cold for adult insects to survive. The adult insects die, but their eggs, or young, survive buried in the soil. When spring arrives, the young insects emerge and become adults ready to breed before winter comes again.

Rhinoceros beetle
(*Megasoma elephas*)

Beetle Car

During the 1940s, the tough, rounded beetle shape inspired the German car manufacturer Volkswagen to produce one of the world's most popular family cars, the VW Beetle. The car's tough outer shell, just like that of a beetle, helped it to achieve a good safety record. The design proved so successful that the Beetle car was recently improved and relaunched.

▲ MOVING FORTRESS

The rhinoceros beetle is very well armoured. Its tough exoskeleton covers and protects its whole body. The cuticle (outer skin) on the head and thorax of this male forms three long points that look like a rhinoceros's horns. These points are used in battles with other males over mates.

15

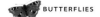
Winged Beauties

Butterflies and moths are the most beautiful of all insects. On sunny days, butterflies flit from flower to flower. Their slow, fluttering flight often reveals the full glory of their large, vividly coloured wings. Moths tend to be less brightly coloured than butterflies and generally fly at night.

Together, butterflies and moths make up one of the largest orders (groups) of insects, called Lepidoptera. This order includes more than 165,000 different species (kinds), living in all parts of the world except Antarctica. Most moths and butterflies feed on sugary flower nectar by dipping a long proboscis (tongue) into the heart of the flower. The proboscis is rolled up under the body when it is not being used.

▼ **RESTING BUTTERFLY**

You can usually tell a butterfly from a moth by the way it folds its wings when it is resting. A moth spreads its wings back like a tent, with only the upper sides visible. However, a butterfly settles with its wings folded upright with the upper sides together, so that only the undersides show.

Geometrid moth
(*Hypochrosis bifurcata*)

Body covered in thick hair

Feathery antennae

▲ **MOTHS**

Most moths fly only at dusk or at night. They rest on tree trunks and in leaf litter by day, where their drab colours make them difficult to see. Moths tend to have plump bodies covered in thick hair, and their feathery antennae are used for sniffing out mates.

Green-veined white butterfly
(*Pieris napi*)

Psyche and Aphrodite
The Ancient Greeks believed that, after death, their souls fluttered away from their bodies in the form of butterflies. The Greek symbol for the soul was a butterfly-winged girl called Psyche. According to legend, Aphrodite (goddess of love) was jealous of Psyche's beauty. She ordered her son Eros to make Psyche fall in love with him. Instead, Eros fell in love with her himself.

Blue morpho butterfly
(*Morpho peleides*)

Antennae

Compound eyes
consist of up to
6,000 individual
lenses.

Brightly coloured
forewing

Wing is
covered in
overlapping
scales that
produce the
bright colours.

Tough outer coating
supports the body,
instead of an
internal skeleton.

Typical slim
body of a
butterfly

The hindwing
is smaller than
the forewing.

▲ FEATURES OF A BUTTERFLY

Butterflies tend to have brilliantly coloured wings
and fly only during the day. They have slim bodies
without much hair, and their antennae are shaped
like clubs, with a lump at the end. However, the
distinction between butterflies and moths is not very
clear, and in some languages they are not
distinguished at all.

▼ CATERPILLARS

A many-legged caterpillar hatches from
a butterfly's egg. When young, both
moths and butterflies are
caterpillars. Only
when they are big
enough do the
caterpillars go
through the
changes that
turn them into
winged adults.

Privet hawk moth caterpillar
(*Sphinx ligustri*)

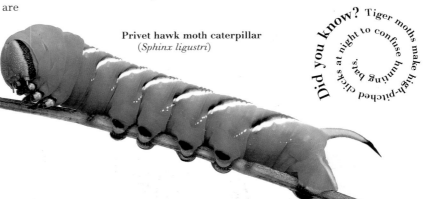

Did you know? Tiger moths make high-pitched clicks at night to confuse hunting bats.

Crawling Creatures

Spiders are some of the most feared and least understood creatures in the animal world. These hairy hunters are famous for spinning silk and giving a poisonous bite. There are around 35,000 known species (kinds) of spider, with probably a similar number waiting to be discovered. Only about 30 species, however, are dangerous to people. Spiders are very useful to humans, because they eat flies and other insect pests that invade our homes and gardens. Spiders live nearly everywhere, from forests, deserts and grasslands to caves. Some even live underwater. Some spin webs to catch their prey, while others leap out from a hiding place or stalk their meals like a cat. There are even spiders that fire streams of sticky silk to tangle up their prey and others that lasso flying moths.

The front part of a spider is a joined head and chest called the cephalothorax. The body is covered by a tough skin called an exoskeleton. The shield-like plate on the top of the cephalothorax is called the carapace and it carries a cluster of small eyes near the front.

Spiders use palps for holding food and as feelers.

The chelicerae (mouthparts) are used to bite and crush prey. Each ends in a fang that injects poison.

A spider's eight hollow legs are joined to the cephalothorax.

The abdomen is the rear part of a spider. It is covered by soft, stretchy skin.

Silk is spun by organs called spinnerets at the back of the abdomen.

◄ WHAT IS A SPIDER?

Spiders are often confused with insects, but they belong to a completely different group. A spider has eight legs, while an insect has six. Its body has two parts, while an insect's has three. Many insects have wings and antennae, but spiders do not.

WEB WEAVERS ▶

About half of all spiders spin webs. They know how to do this by instinct from birth, without being taught. Many spiders build a new web each night. They build webs to catch flying prey. Some of the web's silk is sticky to trap animals. The spider walks around on non-stick strands.

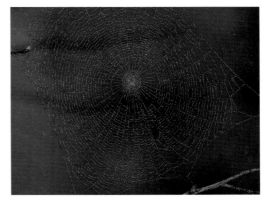

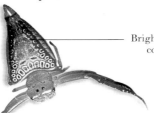

Bright colours help to conceal this spider among flowers.

▲ SPIDER SHAPES AND COLOURS

The triangular spider is named after its brightly coloured abdomen, which is shaped like a triangle. Its colour and shape help it to hide in wait for prey on leaves and flowers. Other spiders use bright colours to warn their enemies that they are poisonous or taste nasty.

Arachne's Tale
A Greek legend tells of Arachne, a girl who was very skilled at weaving. The goddess Athene challenged her to a contest, which Arachne won. The goddess became so cross Arachne killed herself. Athene was sorry and turned the girl into a spider so she could spin forever. The scientific name for spiders is arachnids, named after Arachne.

◀ MALES AND FEMALES

Female spiders are usually bigger than the males and not so colourful, though this female *Nephila* spider is boldly marked. The male at the top of the picture is only one-fifth of her size.

Did you know? All spiders are carnivores (meat-eaters) and many are cannibals.

How Spiders Work

From the outside, a spider's body is very different from ours. It has a tough outer skeleton, called an exoskeleton, and legs that have many joints. It has several eyes and a mouth, but no ears, nose or tongue. Instead, it relies on a variety of hairs and bristles to touch, taste and hear things, and it smells through microscopic pores on its feet. Inside, a spider has many features common to other animals, such as blood, nerves, a brain and a digestive system. It also has special glands for spinning silk and for making and storing poison.

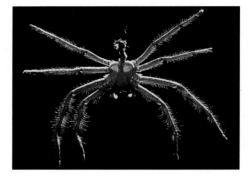

▲ SHEDDING SKIN

A spider's exoskeleton protects its body like a suit of armour. A waxy layer helps to make it waterproof. The exoskeleton cannot stretch as the spider grows so must be shed from time to time after a new, looser skin has grown underneath. The old skin of a huntsman spider is shown here.

Male spiders use taste hairs to pick up scent trails left by females.

◄ HAIRY SIGNALS

The sensitive hairs covering a spider send signals to the brain alerting it to food and enemies. Tasting hairs are spread all over the spider's body. On the palps and legs, special hairs, called trichobothria, set in cup-like sockets pick up movements in the air.

▲ PICKING UP VIBRATIONS

A green orb-weaver devours a fly trapped in the sticky web. Spiders use special slits on their bodies to detect when an insect is trapped in their webs. These slits, called lyriform organs, pick up vibrations caused by a struggling insect. Nerve endings in the slits send signals to the spider's brain.

SPIDER POISON ▶

A spider is a delicate creature compared to some of the prey it catches. By using poison, a spider can kill or paralyse its victim before the latter has a chance to do any harm. The spider pumps poison through its fangs. Spiders cannot chew solid food, and their poison turns the prey's body into a fleshy goo. The spider sucks up this liquid.

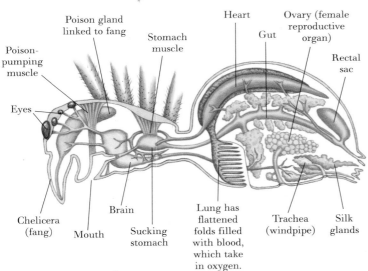

Poison gland linked to fang

Stomach muscle

Poison-pumping muscle

Eyes

Heart

Gut

Ovary (female reproductive organ)

Rectal sac

Chelicera (fang)

Mouth

Brain

Sucking stomach

Lung has flattened folds filled with blood, which take in oxygen.

Trachea (windpipe)

Silk glands

◀ INSIDE A SPIDER

The front part of a spider, the cephalothorax, contains the brain, poison glands and stomach. The abdomen contains the heart, lungs, breathing tubes, gut, waste disposal system, silk glands and reproductive organs. A spider's stomach works like a pump, stretching wide to pull in food that has been turned into a soupy pulp. The heart pumps blue blood around the body.

Raiko and the Earth Spider
People have regarded spiders as dangerous, magical animals for thousands of years. This Japanese print from the 1830s shows the legendary warrior Yorimitsu (also known as Raiko) and his followers slaying the fearsome Earth Spider.

Long, thin, bendy body with no legs

Tough scales protect the body and stop it drying out.

Snake Life

Snakes are reptiles, closely related to lizards and more distantly to crocodiles and turtles. Altogether, there are about 2,700 different kinds of snake, but only 300 or so are able to kill people. In Europe or North America, you are more likely to be struck by lightning than to be bitten by a poisonous snake. All snakes have long bodies covered with waterproof scales. They are meat-eaters and swallow their prey whole. Snakes have always had a special place in myths and legends, being used as symbols of both good and evil.

◀ A SNAKE'S TAIL
The tail of a snake is the part behind a small opening called the cloaca, where the body wastes pass out. The snake narrows slightly where the tail begins.

Tail – the part of the body that tapers off to a point

Grass snake
(*Natrix natrix*)

◀ SNAKE HEADS
Most snakes have a definite head and neck. But in some snakes, one end of the body looks very much like the other end!

Rattlesnake
(*Crotalus*)

◀ FORKED TONGUE

Snakes and some lizards have forked tongues. A snake flicks its tongue out to taste and smell the air. This gives the snake a picture of what is around it. A snake does this every few seconds if it is hunting or if there is any danger nearby.

Colombian rainbow boa
(*Epicrates cenchria maurus*)

▲ SCALY ARMOUR

A covering of tough, dry scales grows out of a snake's skin. The scales usually hide the skin. After a big meal, the skin stretches so that it becomes visible between the scales. A snake's scales protect its body while allowing it to stretch, coil and bend. The scales may be either rough or smooth.

Red-tailed boa
(*Boa constrictor*)

Did you know? Snakes never feel slimy to the touch.

Did you know? A boa squeezes its prey to death in its coils.

Eye has no eyelid.

Forked tongue

Medusa

An ancient Greek myth tells of Medusa, a monster with snakes for hair. Anyone who looked at her was turned to stone. Perseus managed to avoid this fate by using his polished shield to look only at the monster's reflection. He cut off Medusa's head and carried it home, dripping with blood. As each drop touched the earth, it turned into a snake.

Egg-eating snake
(*Dasypeltis fasciata*)

◀ STRETCHY STOMACH

Luckily, the throat and gut of the egg-eating snake are so elastic that its thin body can stretch enough to swallow a whole egg, shell and all. Strong muscles in the throat force food down into the stomach.

Right lung is very long and thin and does the work of two lungs.

Liver is very long and thin.

Inside a Snake

A snake has a stretched-out inside to match its long, thin outside. The backbone extends along the whole body with hundreds of ribs joined to it. There is not much room for organs such as the heart, lungs, kidneys and liver, so they are thin shapes to fit inside the snake's body. Many snakes have only one lung. The stomach and gut are stretchy so that they can hold large meals. When a snake swallows big prey, it pushes the opening of the windpipe forward from the back of its mouth in order to keep breathing. Snakes are cold-blooded, which means that their body temperature is the same as their surroundings.

Flexible tail bone, which extends from the spine

▼ SNAKE ORGANS

This diagram shows the inside of a male snake. The organs are arranged to fit the snake's long shape. In most backboned animals, paired organs, such as the kidneys, are the same size and placed opposite each other.

▲ RATTLER

Rattlesnakes have dried scales on their tail. When cornered, the snake shakes its tail to produce a warning rattle.

Rectum, through which waste is passed to the cloaca

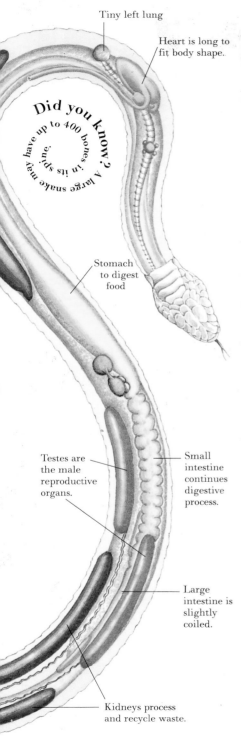

Tiny left lung

Heart is long to fit body shape.

Did you know? A large snake may have up to 400 bones in its spine.

Stomach to digest food

Testes are the male reproductive organs.

Small intestine continues digestive process.

Large intestine is slightly coiled.

Kidneys process and recycle waste.

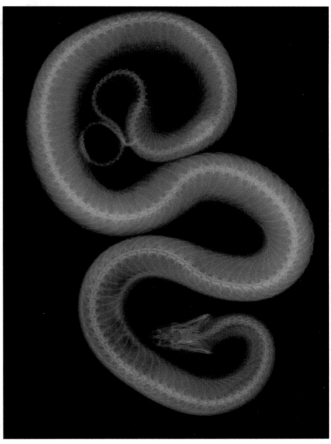

▲ SNAKE BONES

This X-ray of a grass snake shows the delicate bones that make up its skeleton. There are no arm, leg, shoulder or hip bones. The snake's ribs do not extend into the tail.

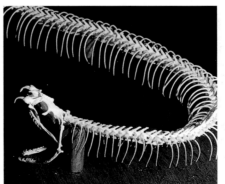

◀ SKELETON

A snake's skeleton is made up of a skull and a spine with ribs arching out from it. The jawbones can be separated so large meals can pass through.

Fierce Creatures

Crocodilians are scaly, armour-clad reptiles that include crocodiles, alligators, caimans and gharials. They are survivors from a prehistoric age – their relatives first lived on the Earth with the dinosaurs nearly 200 million years ago. Today, they are the dinosaurs' closest living relatives, apart from birds.

Crocodilians are fierce predators. They lurk motionless in rivers, lakes and swamps, waiting to snap up prey with their enormous jaws and sharp teeth. Their prey ranges from insects, frogs and fish to birds and large mammals, such as deer and zebras. Crocodilians usually live in warm, tropical places in or near fresh water, but some live in the sea. They hunt and feed mainly in the water, but crawl on to dry land to sunbathe, build nests and lay their eggs. Crocodilians rarely attack humans, even saltwater crocodiles, the largest species.

▲ **SCALY TAILS**
Like many crocodilians, an American alligator uses its long, strong tail to swim through the water. The tail moves from side to side to push the alligator along. The tail is the same length as the rest of the body.

Long, strong tail has flat sides to push aside water for swimming.

The Chinese Dragon
People in China have worshipped the dragon, a mythical creature, for centuries. The original stories surrounding the dragon may have been based on the real-life Chinese alligator. According to ancient texts, the dragon was a supernatural creature that could take on many different forms. It could change instantly from thick to thin or long to short, and could soar into the heavens or plunge to the depths of the sea.

CROCODILIAN CHARACTERISTICS ▶
With its thick, scaly skin, huge jaws and powerful tail, this American alligator looks like a living dinosaur. Its eyes and nostrils are on top of its head so that it can see and breathe when the rest of its body is underwater. On land, crocodilians slither along on their bellies, but they can lift themselves up on their four short legs to walk.

▲ TALKING HEADS

Huge, powerful jaws lined with sharp teeth make Nile crocodiles killing machines. They are some of the world's largest and most dangerous reptiles. The teeth are used to attack and grip prey, but are useless for chewing. Prey has to be swallowed whole or in chunks.

SHUTEYE ▶

Although this spectacled caiman has its eyes shut, it is probably not asleep, just resting. Two butterflies are basking in safety on the caiman's head. Animals will not dare to come near because the caiman is still sensitive to what is going on around it, even though its eyes are shut.

SOAKING UP THE SUN ▶

Nile crocodiles sun themselves on a sandbank. This is called basking and it warms the body. Crocodilians are cold-blooded, which means that their body temperature is affected by their surroundings. They have no fur or feathers to keep them warm, nor can they shiver to warm up. They sunbathe to warm themselves and slip into the water to cool down.

The scales on the back are usually much more bony than those on the belly.

Scaly skin covers the whole body for protection and camouflage.

Did you know? Most crocodilians live for about 50 years but some live up to 100.

Eyes and nostrils are on top of the head.

The digits (toes) of each foot are slightly webbed.

American alligator (*Alligator mississippiensis*)

Long snout with sharp teeth to catch prey

Crocodilian Bodies

The crocodilian body has changed very little over the last 200 million years. It is superbly adapted to life in the water. Crocodilians can breathe with just their nostrils above the surface. Underwater, ears and nostrils close and a transparent third eyelid sweeps across the eye for protection. Crocodilians are the only reptiles with ear flaps. Inside the long, lizard-like body, a bony skeleton supports and protects the lungs, heart, stomach and other soft organs. The stomach is in two parts, one part for grinding food, the other for absorbing (taking in) nutrients. Unlike other reptiles, which have a three-chambered heart, a crocodilian's heart has four chambers, like a mammal's. This stronger heart can pump more oxygen-rich blood to the brain during a dive. The thinking part of its brain is more developed than in other reptiles, and crocodilians learn their hunting skills rather than just acting on instinct.

▲ **THROAT FLAP**
A crocodilian has no lips so it is unable to seal its mouth underwater. Instead, two special flaps at the back of the throat stop water flowing from its mouth into its lungs. This enables the crocodile to open its mouth underwater to catch and eat prey without drowning.

Did you know? A saltwater crocodile can stay underwater for more than an hour.

◄ **OPEN WIDE**
Crocodilians have mighty jaws. However, the muscles that close the mouth are much stronger than the ones that open it. This American alligator is relaxing with its mouth agape. Gaping helps to cool the animal down.

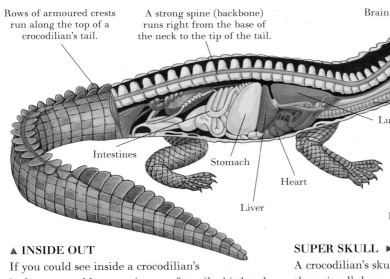

Rows of armoured crests run along the top of a crocodilian's tail.

A strong spine (backbone) runs right from the base of the neck to the tip of the tail.

Brain

Trachea (Windpipe)

Lung

Intestines

Stomach

Heart

Liver

American alligator skull

Eye socket

American crocodile skull

▲ INSIDE OUT

If you could see inside a crocodilian's body, you would see a mixture of reptile, bird and mammal features. The crocodilian's brain and shoulder blades are like a bird's. Its heart, diaphragm and efficient breathing system are similar to those of mammals. The stomach and digestive system are those of a reptile, as they deal with food in unchewed chunks.

SUPER SKULL ▶

A crocodilian's skull protects the animal's large reptile brain. The skull is wider and more rounded in alligators (*top*), and long and triangular in crocodiles (*bottom*). Behind the eye sockets are two large holes where strong jaw muscles emerge and attach to the outer surface of the skull.

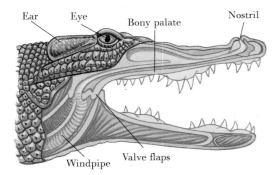

Ear

Eye

Bony palate

Nostril

Windpipe

Valve flaps

▲ WELL DESIGNED

A view inside the head of a crocodilian shows the ear, eye and nostril openings set high up in the skull. The bones in the roof of the mouth are joined together to create a bony palate that separates the nostrils from the mouth. Flaps of skin form a valve, sealing off the windpipe underwater.

▶ STOMACH STONES

Crocodilians swallow objects, such as pebbles, to help mash up their food. These gastroliths (stomach stones) churn around inside part of the stomach, helping to break up food so it can be digested. Not all gastroliths are stones. Bottles, coins and a whistle have been found inside crocodilians.

Winged Hunters

There are nearly 9,000 different species (kinds) of birds in the world. Most of them eat plant shoots, seeds, nuts and fruit, or small creatures such as insects and worms. However, around 400 species, called birds of prey, hunt larger creatures or scavenge carrion (the flesh of dead animals). Birds of prey are called raptors, from the Latin *rapere* meaning 'to seize', because they grip and kill their prey with sharp talons (claws) and hooked beaks. Raptors have very sharp eyes and good hearing, so they can locate their prey on the wing. Most raptors, including eagles, falcons and hawks hunt by day. Vultures are active in the day, too, searching for carrion. Owls are raptors that hunt by night.

▼ HANGING AROUND
The outstretched wings of the kestrel face into the wind as the bird hovers like a kite above a patch of ground in search of a meal. The bird also spreads the feathers of its broad tail to keep it steady in the wind.

Large, forward-facing eyes

Hooked, powerful bill

▼ IN A LEAGUE OF THEIR OWN
Five young tawny owls cluster together on a branch. Owls are not closely related to the other birds of prey. However, like other raptors they have talons, hooked beaks and excellent eyesight. Most hunt silently during the hours of darkness. Their rounded faces act like satellite dishes that collect the slightest sounds and direct them to the birds' ears.

Tawny owls
(*Strix aluco*)

◀ HAWKEYE

The sparrowhawk has large eyes that face forward. The bill is hooked, for tearing flesh. These are typical features of hunters.

Eurasian sparrowhawk
(*Accipiter nisus*)

Wings lift in the flow of air and support the bird's weight. The primary feathers on the wing fan out.

Long, sharp, curved talons

Tail guides the bird through the air and also acts as a brake.

▲ BUILT FOR SPEED

The peregrine falcon is one of the swiftest birds in the world, able to dive at up to 224 km/h. Its swept-back wings help it cut through the air at speed. Their shape has been copied by aircraft designers for the wings of fighter planes.

▼ THE EAGLE HAS LANDED

In the snow-covered highlands of Scotland, a golden eagle stands over a rabbit it has just killed. Eagles kill with their talons which are so long, sharp and deeply curved that one swipe is usually enough to kill the rabbit.

Golden eagle
(*Aquila chrysaetos*)

God of the Sky

Horus was one of the most important gods in ancient Egypt. He was the god of the sky and the heavens. His sacred bird was the falcon, and Horus is often represented with a human body and a falcon's head. The Egyptian hieroglyph (picture symbol) for 'god' in ancient Egyptian is a falcon.

How Birds of Prey Work

Birds of prey are expert fliers. Like other birds, they have powerful chest and wing muscles to move their wings. Virtually the whole body is covered with feathers to make it smooth so that it can slip easily through the air. The bones are very light, and some have a honeycomb structure, which makes them even lighter but still very strong. Birds of prey differ from other birds in a number of ways, particularly in their powerful bills (beaks) and clawed feet, which are well adapted for their life as hunters. Also, like many other birds, they regurgitate (cough up) pellets. These contain the parts of their prey they cannot digest.

▲ **NAKED NECK**
A Ruppell's vulture feeds on a zebra carcass in the Masai Mara region of eastern Africa. Like many vultures, it has a naked neck, which it can thrust deep inside the carcass. As a result, it can feed without getting its feathers too covered in blood.

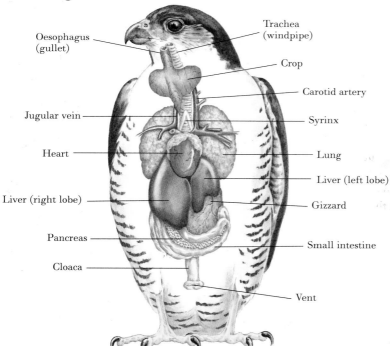

Oesophagus (gullet)

Trachea (windpipe)

Crop

Carotid artery

Jugular vein

Syrinx

Heart

Lung

Liver (left lobe)

Liver (right lobe)

Gizzard

Pancreas

Small intestine

Cloaca

Vent

◄ **BODY PARTS**
Underneath their feathery covering, birds of prey have a complex system of internal organs. Unlike humans, most birds have a crop to store food in before digestion. They also have a gizzard to grind up hard particles of food, such as bone, and to start the process of making a pellet. Birds also have a syrinx (the bird equivalent of the human voice box).

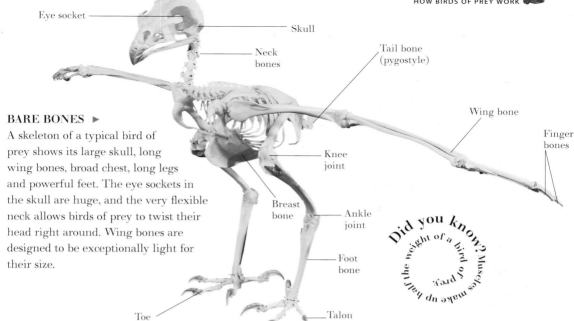

Eye socket

Skull

Neck bones

Tail bone (pygostyle)

Wing bone

Finger bones

BARE BONES ▶

A skeleton of a typical bird of prey shows its large skull, long wing bones, broad chest, long legs and powerful feet. The eye sockets in the skull are huge, and the very flexible neck allows birds of prey to twist their head right around. Wing bones are designed to be exceptionally light for their size.

Knee joint

Breast bone

Ankle joint

Foot bone

Toe

Talon

Did you know? Muscles make up half the weight of a bird of prey.

▼ BACK TO FRONT

This peregrine falcon appears to have eyes in the back of its head. Its body is facing away, but its eyes are looking straight into the camera. All birds of prey can twist their heads right around like this, because they have many more neck bones than mammals. They can see in any direction without moving their body, but they cannot move their eyeballs in their sockets.

Peregrine falcon
(*Falco peregrinus*)

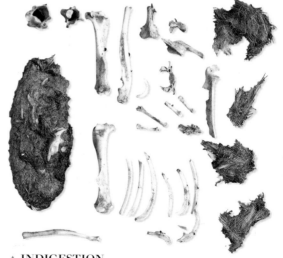

▲ INDIGESTION

On the left of the picture above is the regurgitated (coughed-up) pellet of a barn owl, and on the right are the indigestible parts it contained. The pellet is about 5cm long. From the scraps of fur and fragments of bone in it, we can tell that the owl has just eaten a small mammal.

Built for Speed

Equids are designed to be able to flee from predators. Their skeletons are lightweight, strong and geared for maximum speed with minimum energy. A horse's upper leg bones, for example, are fused into a single, strong bone, while in humans their equivalents are two separate bones. The joints are less flexible than those of a human. Instead, they are strong in an up-and-down direction to support and protect powerful tendons and muscles. A horse's skeleton is designed to absorb the weight and impact of its body as it moves over the ground.

▲ RESTING ON AUTOMATIC
When horses are standing at rest, the patella (kneecap) slots into a groove in the femur (leg bone). This locks their back legs into an energy-saving position, just like our knees. Another mechanism keeps the horse's head from dropping to the ground. A ligament in the neck acts like a piece of elastic, returning the head to an upright resting position when the horse is not grazing.

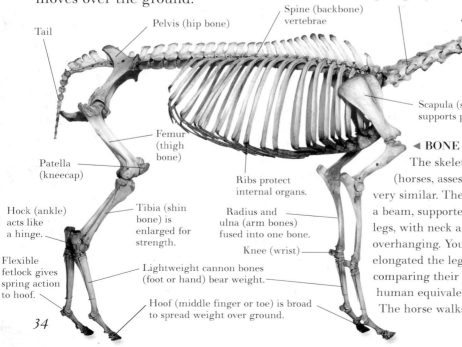

Long neck vertebrae make grazing easy.

Long, narrow skull

Spine (backbone) vertebrae

Tail

Pelvis (hip bone)

Scapula (shoulder blade) supports powerful leg muscles.

Femur (thigh bone)

Patella (kneecap)

Ribs protect internal organs.

◀ BONE STRUCTURE
The skeletons of all equids (horses, asses and zebras) are very similar. The backbone is like a beam, supported on long, slender legs, with neck and head overhanging. You can see how elongated the leg bones are by comparing their position with the human equivalents (in brackets). The horse walks on tiptoe.

Hock (ankle) acts like a hinge.

Tibia (shin bone) is enlarged for strength.

Radius and ulna (arm bones) fused into one bone.

Knee (wrist)

Flexible fetlock gives spring action to hoof.

Lightweight cannon bones (foot or hand) bear weight.

Hoof (middle finger or toe) is broad to spread weight over ground.

34

◀ SPACE FOR CHEWING

The long and narrow skull provides space for the big molar teeth, and enables the eye sockets to fit in behind them. This means that when the horse chews, there is no pressure on the eye. The large eye sockets give enough space for the horse to have all-round vision.

▼ FIGHTING TEETH

The small tushes (or tusker) teeth, just behind the big incisors, are used in fights between stallions (males). Mares (females) have very small tushes teeth or none at all.

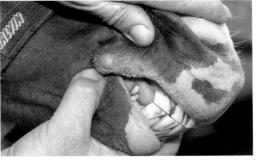

Pegasus

Greek mythology tells of a winged horse called Pegasus. He sprang fully grown from the dead body of the evil Medusa after she was beheaded. Pegasus was ridden by the hero Bellerophon. Together they defeated the fire-breathing monster, the Chimera. Bellerophon tried to ride Pegasus to heaven but the gods were angry and he was thrown off and killed. Pegasus became a constellation in the night sky.

TEETH FOR THE JOB ▶

Mares have 36–40 teeth and stallions 44 teeth. A horse's teeth are specially adapted for its diet. Chisel-shaped incisors at the front snip through grass. Molars in the side of the mouth grind down the grass before it is swallowed. The degree of wear on teeth is sometimes used to calculate a horse's age. This can be misleading, as some foods wear down the teeth more than others do.

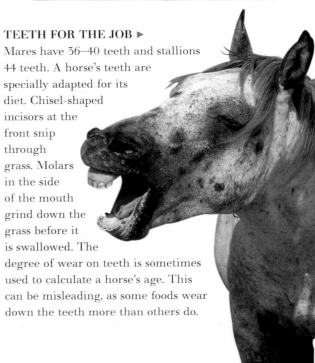

Powerful Bodies

The horse is one of the fastest long-distance runners in the animal world. Its digestive system processes large quantities of food in order to extract sufficient energy. The digestive system is in two parts. The food is partly digested in the stomach, then moves quickly through to the hindgut (cecum and colon). Here, bacteria break down the tough cell walls of the plants. The nutrients are released, and cells lining the gut are ready to absorb them.

Equids also have a big heart and large lungs. This allows them to run quickly and over a long distance. Horse tendons connecting muscles to bones are very elastic, especially those in the lower leg. Together with the ligaments, which bind bones together at joints, they can stretch and give to save energy and cushion impact of the hooves on the ground when the horse is on the move.

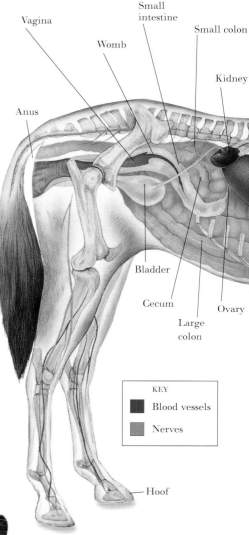

Vagina
Small intestine
Womb
Small colon
Kidney
Anus
Bladder
Cecum
Large colon
Ovary
Hoof

KEY	
■	Blood vessels
■	Nerves

◄ FLEXIBLE LIPS
The horse's mobile, sensitive lips are described as prehensile (able to grasp). They are used to select and pick food. When a horse wants to use its power of smell to full effect, it curls its lips back.

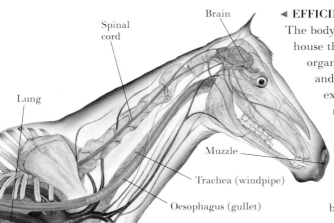

Spinal cord

Brain

Lung

Muzzle

Trachea (windpipe)

Oesophagus (gullet)

Heart

Liver

Stomach

Spleen

◀ **EFFICIENT BODYWORKS**

The body of the horse is big enough to house the powerful muscles and large organs that the animal needs for speed and endurance. The large heart, for example, pumps at 30–40 beats per minute when resting – about half the rate of a human's. This can rise to a top rate of 240 – nearly twice the rate of a human's – when working hard. This means that blood circulates around the body very efficiently.

ONE WAY TRIP ▶

Horses eat almost continuously, and have an extra-long digestive tract – around 30m – to get as much benefit as possible from their low-grade diet. They cannot vomit because one-way valves in the stomach prevent food from being regurgitated. Eating something poisonous could, therefore, be fatal.

LONG LEGS ▶

Horses' feet have a single toe, tipped with a fingernail-like hoof. Horses stand on this single toe. Their heel bone never touches the ground, making their legs very long – ideal for running and jumping.

Gentle Giants

Elephants are the largest and heaviest creatures on land. An African male (bull) elephant weighs as much as 80 people, six cars, 12 large horses or 1,500 cats. Elephants are extremely strong and can pick up whole trees with their trunks. They are also highly intelligent, gentle animals. Females live together in family groups and look after one another. Elephants are mammals — they can control their body temperature and they feed milk to their babies. After humans, elephants are the longest lived of all mammals. Some live to be about 70 years old. Two species (kinds) of elephant exist today — the African elephant and the Asian elephant. Both have a trunk, thick skin and large ears, although African elephants have larger ears than Indian ones. Not all elephants have tusks, however. Generally, only African elephants and male Asian elephants have tusks.

▲ **WORKING ELEPHANTS**
In India, domesticated (tamed) elephants are used by farmers to carry heavy loads. In some Asian countries they also move heavy logs by pulling them.

African elephant (*Loxodonta africana*)

Tail, has a brush of thick hair at the end.

Indra and the Elephant
One of the most celebrated Hindu gods, Indra, rides a mighty white elephant called Airavata. In Hinduism (the main religion of India), elephants are sacred animals. One of Indra's emblems is the ankus, a special pointed stick used to control elephants. Indra is shown holding an ankus in this painting.

▼ UNUSUAL FEATURES

The mighty elephant is a record-breaking beast. Not only is it the largest land animal, it is also the second tallest (only the giraffe is taller). It has larger ears, teeth and tusks than any other animal. The elephant is also one of the few animals to have a nose in the form of a long trunk.

FAMILY LIFE ▲

Adult male and female elephants do not live together in family groups. Instead, adult sisters and daughters live in groups led by an older female. Adult males (bulls) live on their own or in all-male groups.

Huge ear is flapped to keep the elephant cool.

Small eyes are protected by long eyelashes.

BABY ELEPHANTS ▲

An elephant baby feels safe between its mother's front legs. It spends most of the first year of its life there. Mother elephants look after their young for longer than any other animal parent except humans. Daughters never leave the family group unless the group becomes too big.

Wrinkly skin has hardly any hair.

Long trunk is used as a nose and for lifting things.

Gently curved tusks are used for digging, fighting and lifting.

Strong legs and flat feet give support.

Elephant Bodies

An elephant's skin is thick, grey and wrinkly, and surprisingly sensitive. Some insects, including flies and mosquitoes, can bite through it. Often, elephants roll around in the mud to keep flies from biting them (as well as cooling themselves down). Underneath the skin, the elephant has typical mammal body parts, only very large. The heart, for example, is about five times bigger than a human heart and weighs up to 21kg — the weight of a small child. Also, an elephant's huge intestines can weigh nearly a tonne, including the contents. The powerful lungs are operated by strong muscles. These let the elephant breathe underwater while using its trunk as a snorkel.

▲ THICK SKIN
An elephant's skin is 2.5cm thick on the back and in some areas of the head. But in other places, such as around the mouth, the skin is paper thin.

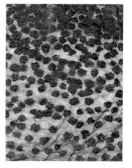

▲ PINK SKIN
An elephant gets its colour from dots of grey pigment (colouring) in the skin. As it ages, this grey pigment may gradually fade so that the skin looks pink.

Did you know? Some very rare Asian elephants have white skin.

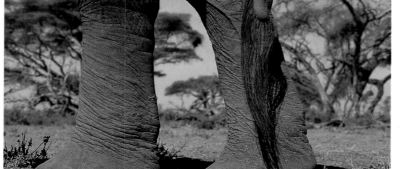

◄ ELEPHANT HAIR
The hairiest part of an elephant is the end of its tail. The tail hairs are many times thicker than human hair and grow into thick tufts. Apart from the end of the tail, the chin and around the eyes and ears, the adult elephant has very little hair.

▲ FLY SWATTER

Although they can swish their tufted tails to get rid of flies, elephants also use leafy branches to swat annoying insect pests. They pick a branch up with their trunks and brush it across their backs to wipe the pests away.

Flying Elephants

According to an Indian folk tale, elephants could once fly. This ability was taken away by a hermit with magical powers when a flock of elephants woke him from a deep trance. The elephants landed in a tree above him, making a lot of noise and causing a branch to fall on his head. The hermit was so furious that he cast a magical spell.

▼ INSIDE AN ELEPHANT

If you could look inside the body of an elephant, you would see its huge skeleton supporting the organs. The cross-section shown here is of a female African elephant.

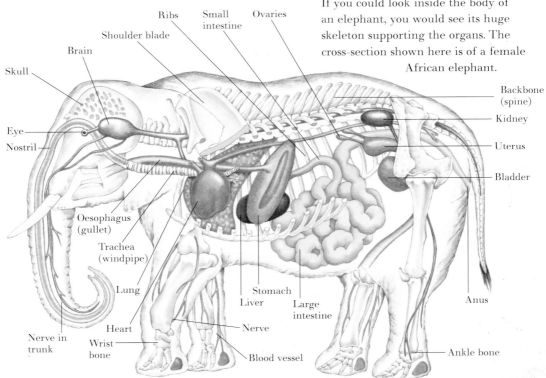

Ribs

Small intestine

Ovaries

Shoulder blade

Brain

Skull

Eye

Nostril

Backbone (spine)

Kidney

Uterus

Bladder

Oesophagus (gullet)

Trachea (windpipe)

Lung

Stomach

Liver

Large intestine

Heart

Nerve

Anus

Nerve in trunk

Wrist bone

Blood vessel

Ankle bone

41

Big Bones

An elephant's legs are placed directly underneath its body, like a table's legs. This arrangement provides a firm support for its great weight. The leg bones stack one above the other to form a strong pillar. As a result, an elephant can rest, and even sleep, while standing up. The pillar-like legs also help to hold up the backbone, which runs along the top of the animal and supports the ribs. The backs of Asian elephants arch upwards, while African elephants' backs have a dip in them. These different shapes are produced by bones that stick up from the backbone. The elephant's skeleton is not just built for strength, however. It is also flexible enough to let the elephant kneel and squat.

▲ **BONY BACK**
Crests of bone stick up from the backbone of the Asian elephant's skeleton. The muscles that hold up the head are joined to these spines and to the back of the skull.

Elephant's skull

Large eye socket

Start of tusk

▲ **CAGED IN**
The skull is the bony box that protects the brain and holds the huge teeth and tusks. The skull above is that of a young male elephant with undeveloped tusks. On an adult male, the upper jaw juts out farther than the lower jaw because it contains the roots for the heavy tusks.

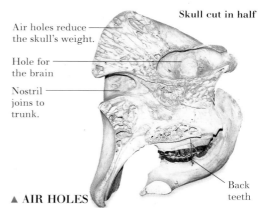

Skull cut in half

Air holes reduce the skull's weight.

Hole for the brain

Nostril joins to trunk.

Back teeth

▲ **AIR HOLES**
An elephant has a large skull compared to the size of its body. However, a honeycomb of air holes inside the skull makes it lighter than it looks from the outside.

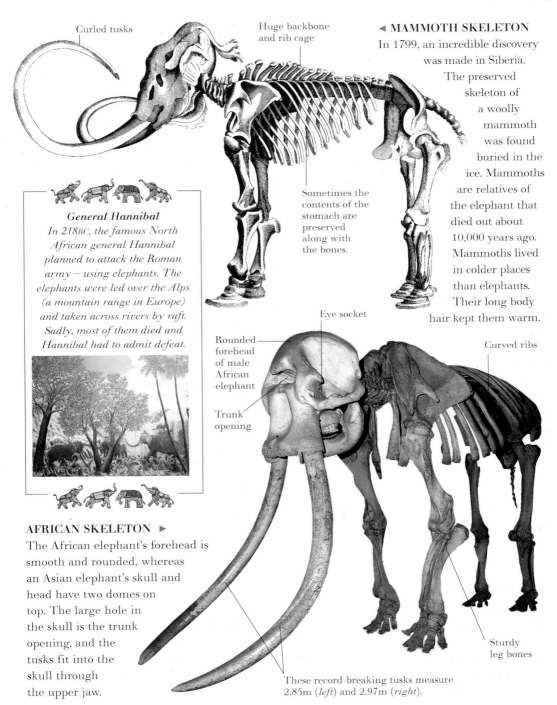

Curled tusks

Huge backbone
and rib cage

◄ **MAMMOTH SKELETON**

In 1799, an incredible discovery
was made in Siberia.
The preserved
skeleton of
a woolly
mammoth
was found
buried in the
ice. Mammoths
are relatives of
the elephant that
died out about
10,000 years ago.
Mammoths lived
in colder places
than elephants.
Their long body
hair kept them warm.

Sometimes the
contents of the
stomach are
preserved
along with
the bones.

General Hannibal

*In 218BC, the famous North
African general Hannibal
planned to attack the Roman
army – using elephants. The
elephants were led over the Alps
(a mountain range in Europe)
and taken across rivers by raft.
Sadly, most of them died and
Hannibal had to admit defeat.*

Eye socket

Curved ribs

Rounded
forehead
of male
African
elephant

Trunk
opening

AFRICAN SKELETON ►

The African elephant's forehead is
smooth and rounded, whereas
an Asian elephant's skull and
head have two domes on
top. The large hole in
the skull is the trunk
opening, and the
tusks fit into the
skull through
the upper jaw.

Sturdy
leg bones

These record-breaking tusks measure
2.85m (*left*) and 2.97m (*right*).

43

The Bear Facts

Bears may look cuddly and appealing, but in reality they are enormously powerful animals. Bears are mammals with bodies covered in thick fur. They are heavily built with a short tail and large claws. All bears are basically carnivores (meat-eaters), but most enjoy a very mixed diet with just the occasional snack of meat. The exception is the polar bear, which feasts on the blubber (fat) of seals. There are eight species (kinds) of bear: the brown or grizzly bear, American black bear, Asiatic black bear, polar bear, sun bear, sloth bear, spectacled bear and giant panda. They live in both cold and tropical regions of the world. The sun bears of South-east Asia are the smallest at 1.5m long, while Alaska's brown bears are the largest at 2.7m long.

Winnie-the-Pooh
The lovable teddy bear Winnie-the-Pooh was created by A.A. Milne. Like real bears he loves honey. Teddy bears became popular as toys in the early 1900s. The President of the USA, Teddy Roosevelt refused to shoot a bear cub on a hunting trip. Toy bears went on sale soon after known as "Teddy's bears".

◄ **BEAR FACE**
The brown bear shares the huge dog-like head and face of all bears. Bears have prominent noses, but relatively small eyes and ears. This is because they mostly rely on their sense of smell to help them find food.

▲ **BIG FLAT FEET**
A polar bear's feet are broad, flat and furry. The five long, curved claws cannot be retracted (pulled back). One swipe could kill a seal instantly.

Thick fur covers a
heavily built body.

A bear's main
strength is in its
massive shoulders
and front legs.

Its broad, flat feet
have long claws.

◀ POINTS OF A BEAR

The brown bear is called the grizzly
bear in North America. Fully-grown
brown bears weigh nearly half a tonne.
They fear no other animals apart from
humans. They can chase prey at high
speed, but they rarely bother as
they feed mainly on plants.

A bear has a large head,
with small eyes and
erect, rounded ears.

The long, prominent,
dog-like snout
dominates the face.

▲ GIANT PANDA

China's giant panda, with its distinctive
black and white face, is a very unusual
bear. Unlike most other bears, which
will eat anything, pandas feed almost
exclusively on the bamboo plant.

◀ ARCTIC NOMAD

Most bears lead a solitary life. The polar bear
wanders alone across the Arctic sea ice.
Usually it will not tolerate other
bears. The exceptions are
bears that congregate at
rubbish dumps, or
mothers accompanied
by their cubs, as
shown here.

45

Bear Bodies

Bears are the bully-boys of the animal
kingdom, using their size, strength and
deep roar to scare off other animals. Most
species (kinds) can stand up on their back
legs for a short time to make themselves
look even more fierce. At other times, a
bear will put its powerful forelimbs to
good use in digging, climbing, fishing and
fighting. Bears do not like each other's
company and will often attack other bears
that cross their path. During fights, bears
can do considerable damage with their
teeth and claws and survive by sheer brute
force. Male bears are generally much
larger than females of the same species.

▲ **CLAWS DOWN**
The sun bear has particularly large,
curved claws for climbing trees. It
spends most of the day sleeping or
sunbathing in the branches. At night it
strips off bark with its claws, looking for
insects and honey in bees' nests.

◄ **PUTTING ON WEIGHT**
This grizzly bear is at peak size. Most bears change size as
the seasons pass. They are large and well-fed in autumn,
ready for their winter hibernation. When they emerge
in spring, they are scrawny with sagging coats.

Beowulf
*An Anglo-Saxon poem tells of the hero
Beowulf (bear-wolf). He had the
strength of a bear and went through
many heroic adventures. Beowulf is
famous for slaying a monster
called Grendel. Here, Beowulf
as an old man lies dying
from the wounds inflicted
by a fire-breathing dragon.*

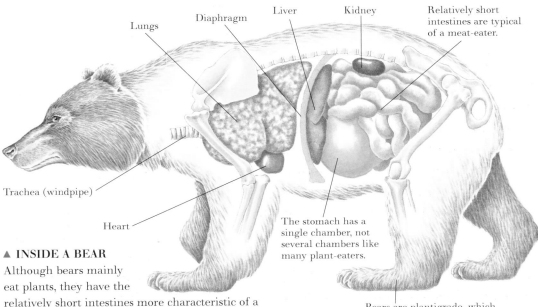

Lungs

Diaphragm

Liver

Kidney

Relatively short intestines are typical of a meat-eater.

Trachea (windpipe)

Heart

The stomach has a single chamber, not several chambers like many plant-eaters.

Bears are plantigrade, which means they walk on the soles of their feet.

▲ INSIDE A BEAR

Although bears mainly eat plants, they have the relatively short intestines more characteristic of a meat-eater, rather than a long gut like a cow. This makes it hard for them to digest their food. Curiously, the bamboo-eating giant panda has the shortest gut of all. Because of this it can digest no more than 20 per cent of what it eats, compared to 60 per cent in a cow.

▲ SHORT BURSTS

Bears are not particularly agile and swift, but they can run fast over short distances. The brown bear can charge at 50km/h (lions reach about 65km/h) and does sometimes chase its food. A bear at full charge is a frightening sight.

▲ SWEET TOOTH

The sun bear's long slender tongue is ideal for licking honey from bees' nests and for scooping up termites and other insects. Like all bears, it has mobile lips, a flexible snout and strong jaws.

Stealthy Hunters

Cats are native to every continent except Australia and Antarctica. They are mammals with fine fur that is often beautifully marked. All cats are meat-eaters, being skilled hunters and killers with strong agile bodies, acute senses and sharp teeth and claws. Cats are stealthy and intelligent animals, and most kinds live alone and are very secretive. Although cats vary in size from the domestic (house) cats kept by people as pets to the huge Siberian tiger, both wild and domestic cats share many features and behave in very similar ways. In all, there are 38 different species (kinds) of cat.

▲ LONG TAIL
A cat's long tail helps it to balance as it runs. Cats also use their tails to signal their feelings to other cats.

Only male lions have manes – hairy heads and necks.

Whiskers help a cat feel its surroundings.

The body of a cat is muscular and supple, with a broad, powerful chest.

▲ BIG BITE
As this tiger yawns, it reveals its sharp teeth and strong jaws which can give a lethal bite. Cats use these long canine teeth for killing prey.

▲ PRIDE KING
Unlike other cats, most lions live in groups called prides. Each pride is ruled by a single large adult male. The other adult members are all lionesses (females). The lionesses hunt as a team, usually at dusk. Most lions live in the grasslands of Africa, where they feed on large antelopes, such as wildebeests and gazelles.

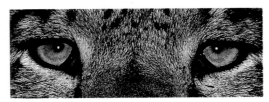

▲ NIGHT SIGHT

The pupils (dark centres) of cats' eyes close to a slit or small circle during the day to keep out the glare. At night they open up to let in as much light as possible. This enables a cat to see clearly at night as well as during the day.

The Lion and the Saint
St Jerome was a Christian scholar who lived from about AD331 to 420. According to legend, he found an injured lion in the desert with a thorn in its paw. Instead of attacking him, the lion befriended the saint when he removed the thorn. St Jerome is often shown with a lion sitting at his feet.

Very soft fur is kept clean by regular grooming with the tongue and paws.

A cat's long tail helps it to balance when leaping on prey.

Cats walk on their toes, not on the whole foot.

Large ears draw in sounds.

Did you know? Some Arctic cultures believe that cats represent the spirits of the dead.

CAT'S EARS ▶

A cat's ears are set high on its head. This gives a keen hunter the best possible chance of picking up sounds. Cats can also swivel their ears to pick up sounds from almost any direction.

Inside a Cat

The skeleton of a cat gives it its shape and has about 230 bones (a human has 206). A cat's short and round skull is joined to the backbone (spine), which supports the body. Vertebrae (bones of the spine) protect the spinal cord, which is the main nerve cable in the body. The ribs are joined to the spine, forming a cage that protects a cat's heart and lungs. Cats' teeth are designed for killing and chewing. Wild cats have to be very careful not to damage their teeth, because with broken teeth they would quickly die from starvation.

Backbone
(spine)

A big, flexible
rib cage has
13 pairs
of ribs.

The number of
bones in the tail
varies according to
the species. Tigers
have 23 – 26, but
cheetahs have 28.

The bones of a cat's
powerful hind legs
are longer than the
front leg bones.

▲ THE FRAME

The powerfully built skeleton of a tiger is similar to all cats' skeletons. Cats have short necks with seven compressed vertebrae. These help to streamline and balance the cat so that it can run at great speeds. All cats have slightly different shoulder bones. A cheetah has long shoulder bones to which sprinting muscles are attached. A leopard, however, has short shoulder bones and thicker, tree-climbing muscles.

◀ CANINES AND CARNASSIALS

A tiger reveals its fearsome teeth. Its long, curved canines are adapted to fit between the neck bones of its prey to break the spinal cord. Like all carnivores, cats have strong back teeth, called carnassials. These teeth work like scissors, slicing through meat.

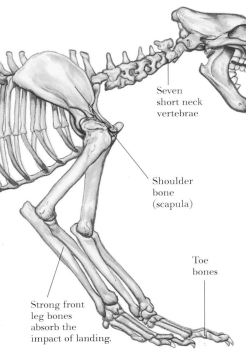

Seven
short neck
vertebrae

Shoulder
bone
(scapula)

Toe
bones

Strong front
leg bones
absorb the
impact of landing.

LANDING FEET ▶

As it falls, this cat twists its supple, flexible spine to make sure its feet will be in the right place for landing. Cats almost always land on their feet when they fall. This helps them to avoid injury as they leap on prey or jump from a tree.

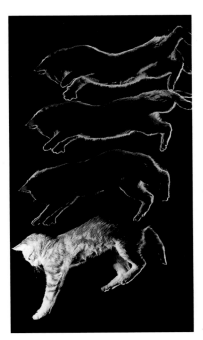

▼ CHEWING ON A BONE

Ravenous lions feast on the carcass of their latest kill. Cats' jaws are hinged so that their jaw bones can move only up and down. Because of this, cats eat on one side of their mouths at a time and they often tilt their heads when they eat.

▼ CAT SKULL

Like all cats' skulls, this tiger's skull has a high crown at the back giving lots of space for the attachment of its strong neck muscles. The eye sockets hold large eyes that allow it to see well to the sides as well as to the front. Its short jaws can open wide to deliver a powerful bite.

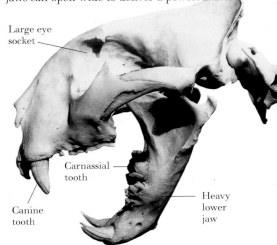

Large eye
socket

Carnassial
tooth

Canine
tooth

Heavy
lower
jaw

51

Killing Machines

Both inside and out, cats are designed to be killers. Thick back and shoulder muscles make them powerful jumpers and climbers. Long, dagger-like teeth and sharp, curved claws that grow from all of their digits (toes) are their weapons. One of the digits on a cat's front foot is called the dew claw. This is held off the ground to keep it sharp and ready to hold prey. Cats are warm-blooded, which means that their bodies stay at the same temperature no matter how hot or cold the weather is. The fur on their skin keeps them warm when conditions are cold. When it is hot, cats cool down by sweating through their noses and paw pads.

Hercules and the Nemean Lion
The mythical Greek hero Hercules was the son of the god Zeus and tremendously strong. As a young man he committed a terrible crime. Part of his punishment was to kill the Nemean lion. The lion had impenetrable skin and could not be killed with arrows or spears. Hercules chased the lion into a cave and strangled it with his hands. He wore its skin as a shield and its head as a helmet.

▼ KNOCKOUT CLAWS

Cheetahs have well-developed dew claws that stick out from their front legs. They use these claws to knock down prey before grabbing its throat or muzzle to finish it off. Other cats use their dew claws to grip while climbing or to hold on to prey. Cats have five claws, including the dew claw, on their front paws. On their back paws, they have only four claws.

Dew claw

Dew claw

Did you know? Cats cannot digest sugar, so they prefer not to eat sweet things.

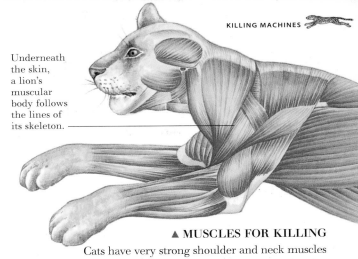

Underneath the skin, a lion's muscular body follows the lines of its skeleton.

▲ TIGER CLAW

This is the extended claw of a tiger. Cats' claws are made of keratin, just like human fingernails. They need to be kept sharp all the time.

▲ MUSCLES FOR KILLING

Cats have very strong shoulder and neck muscles which give it power to attack prey. The muscles also absorb some of the impact when the cat pounces.

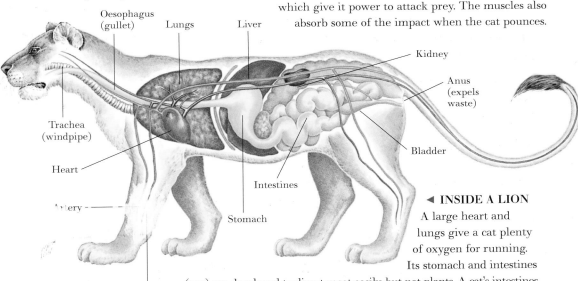

Oesophagus (gullet)

Lungs

Liver

Kidney

Anus (expels waste)

Trachea (windpipe)

Heart

Bladder

Artery

Intestines

Vein

Stomach

◄ INSIDE A LION

A large heart and lungs give a cat plenty of oxygen for running. Its stomach and intestines (gut) are developed to digest meat easily, but not plants. A cat's intestines are quite short, so food passes through quickly. This means as soon as it needs more food, a cat is light enough to run and pounce. However, once a lion has had a big meal, it does not need to eat again for several days.

CLAW PROTECTION ►

Cats retract (pull back) their claws into fleshy sheaths to protect them. This prevents them from getting blunt or damaged. Only cheetahs do not have sheaths.

Sheathed claw is protected by a fleshy covering.

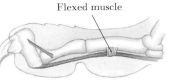

Flexed muscle

The claw is unsheathed when a muscle tightens.

Running Wild

Wolves are wild members of the dog family (canids). They have gleaming yellow eyes and lean, muscular bodies. The 37 different species (kinds) of canids include jackals, coyotes, foxes and wild and domestic dogs, as well as wolves. Canids are native to every continent except Australia and Antarctica. All of them share a keen sense of smell and hearing, and are carnivores (meat-eaters). Wolves and wild dogs hunt live prey, which they kill with their sharp teeth. However, many canids also eat vegetable matter and even insects. They are among the most intelligent of all animals. Many, including the wolves, are highly social animals that live together in groups called packs.

Large, triangular ears, usually held pricked (erect)

Powerful shoulders and supple body

▲ PRODUCING YOUNG
A female wolf suckles (feeds) her cubs. All canids are mammals and feed their young on milk. Females produce a litter of cubs, or pups, once a year. Most are born in an underground den.

BODY FEATURES ▶
The wolf is the largest wild dog. It has a strong, well-muscled body covered with dense, shaggy fur, a long, bushy tail and strong legs made for running. Its muzzle (nose and jaws) is long and well developed and its ears are large. Male and female wolves look very similar, although females are generally the smaller of the two.

54

◄ KEEN SENSES

The jackal, like all dogs, has very keen senses. Its nose can detect faint scents and its large ears pick up the slightest sound. Smell and hearing are mainly used for hunting. Many canids also have good vision.

The Big, Bad Wolf

Fairy tales often depict wolves as wicked, dangerous animals. In the tale of the Three Little Pigs, the big, bad wolf terrorizes three small pigs. Eventually he is outwitted by the smartest pig, who builds a brick house that the wolf cannot blow down, and all the pigs are safe.

Thick, coarse fur helps to protect the wolf from extremes of temperature.

Long, bushy tail

Strong, powerful, muscular legs

Canids walk on all fours on the pads of their toes.

▲ LIVING IN PACKS

Wolves and many other wild dogs live in groups called packs of about eight to 20. Each pack has a hierarchy (social order) and is led by the strongest male and female.

EXPERT HUNTERS ►

A wolf bares its teeth in a snarl to defend its kill. Wolves and other canids feed mainly on meat, but eat plants, too, particularly when they are hungry.

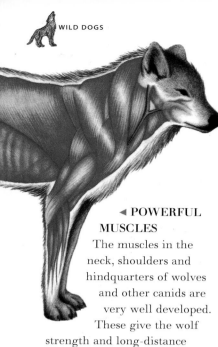

Body of a Wild Dog

Muscular, fast-running wolves and wild dogs are built for chasing prey in open country. Thick muscles and long, strong legs enable them to run fast over great distances. The long muzzle helps the wolf to seize prey on the run. The wolf has a large stomach that can digest meat quickly and hold a big meal after a successful hunt. Wolves, however, can also go without food for more than a week if prey is scarce. Teeth are a wolf's main weapon, used for biting enemies, catching prey and tearing food. Small incisors (front teeth) strip flesh off bones. Long fangs (canines) grab and hold prey. Toward the back, jagged carnassial teeth close together like shears to slice meat into small pieces, while large molars can crush bones.

◄ **POWERFUL MUSCLES**
The muscles in the neck, shoulders and hindquarters of wolves and other canids are very well developed. These give the wolf strength and long-distance stamina as well as speed. When hunting, a wolf pack chases its prey, such as a large deer, until the victim is totally exhausted. Then the pack bites the animal to death.

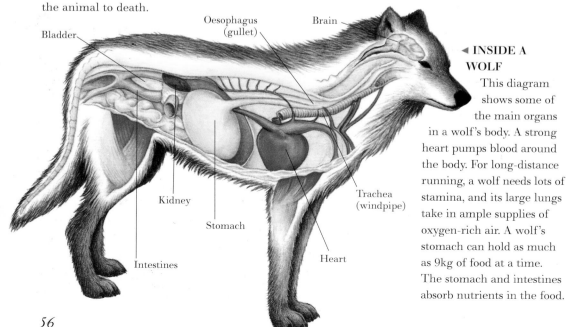

Bladder

Oesophagus (gullet)

Brain

Kidney

Stomach

Trachea (windpipe)

Intestines

Heart

◄ **INSIDE A WOLF**
This diagram shows some of the main organs in a wolf's body. A strong heart pumps blood around the body. For long-distance running, a wolf needs lots of stamina, and its large lungs take in ample supplies of oxygen-rich air. A wolf's stomach can hold as much as 9kg of food at a time. The stomach and intestines absorb nutrients in the food.

▼ WOLF'S SKULL

A wolf's head has a broad crown and a tapering muzzle. The bones of the skull are strong and heavy. They form a tough case that protects the animal's brain, eyes, ears and nose. The jaws have powerful muscles that can exert great pressure as the wolf sinks its teeth into its prey.

molar carnassial canine incisor

▼ BAT-EARED FOX SKULL

The bat-eared fox has a delicate, tapering muzzle. Its jaws are weaker than a wolf's and suited to deal with smaller prey, such as insects. This fox has 46–50 teeth, which is more than any other canid. Extra molars at the back of the animal's mouth enable it to crunch insects, such as beetles, which have a tough outer casing on their bodies.

molar carnassial canine incisor

▲ TIME FOR BED

A wolf shows its full set of meat-eating teeth as it yawns. Wolves and most other canids have 42 teeth. In wolves, the four large, dagger-like canines at the front of the mouth can grow up to 5cm long.

COOLING DOWN ▶

Like all mammals, the wolf is warm-blooded. This means that its body temperature remains constant whatever the weather, so it is always ready to spring into action. Wolves do not have sweat glands all over their bodies as humans do, so in hot weather they cannot sweat to cool down. When the wolf gets too hot, it opens its mouth and pants with its tongue lolling out. Moisture evaporates from the nose, mouth and tongue to cool the animal down.

Monkey Power

The primates are a group of mammals that include monkeys, apes and also humans. Many of them have large brains and are among the most intelligent of animals, but their bodies are still largely the same as those of most other mammals. Small primate bodies are built for flexibility and agility, with hinged joints supported by long, elastic muscles to allow maximum range of movement. Body shapes vary according to whether the animals climb and leap through trees or move along the ground. Head shape and size depend on whether brainpower or the sense of smell or sight is top priority.

▲ DENTAL PRACTICE
Monkeys and prosimians (monkey relatives) have four types of teeth – incisors for cutting, canines for stabbing and ripping, and molars and premolars for grinding tough leaves and fruit into a paste.

▼ INTERNAL VIEW
A monkey's bones and strong muscles protect the vital organs inside its body. Its facial muscles allow it to make expressions. Monkey legs are generally shorter in relation to their bodies than lemur legs. This gives them more precise climbing and reaching skills, especially in the treetops.

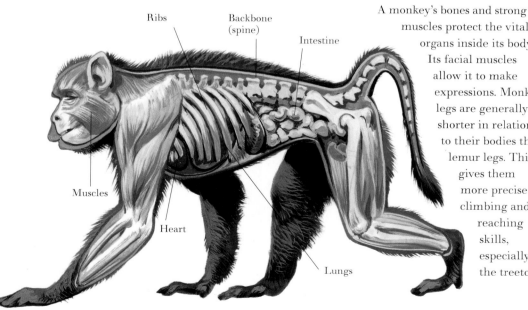

Ribs

Backbone
(spine)

Intestine

Muscles

Heart

Lungs

▼ BIG EYES

The tarsier has the biggest eyes of any animal in relation to its body size. There is not much room left in its skull for a brain and each of the eyes is heavier than the brain. Prosimians have simpler lives than monkeys and do not need big brains. Instead, they have an array of sharp senses — more sensitive than a monkey's — that help them to survive. As well as its huge eyes, this tarsier has large ears that pick up the slightest sounds in the quiet of the night.

▲ A STRONG STOMACH

A baboon's digestive system can cope with raw meat as well as plant food. These big monkeys catch and eat rodents, hares and even small antelopes as well as lots of insects. Most monkeys and prosimians eat mainly plants and have relatively large stomachs and long guts because leaves and other plant foods are hard to digest.

INSIDE LOOK AT A LEMUR ▶

Lemurs belong to a group of monkey relatives called prosimians. These are less advanced than the monkeys. This skeleton of a ruffed lemur has a long, narrow head, which has less space for the brain, and its legs are very long compared to the length of its body. Their long legs help lemurs to leap great distances from tree to tree and enable them to cling in a relaxed fashion to vertical tree trunks.

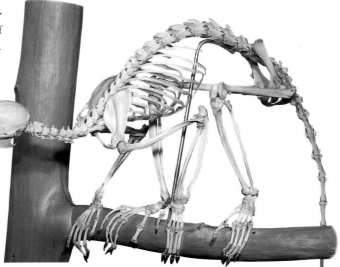

What is a Great Ape?

The four great apes – the chimpanzee, bonobo, gorilla and orangutan – look similar to us because they are our closest animal relatives. Humans are sometimes called the fifth great ape. Great apes are also closely related to the lesser apes, called gibbons. Nearly 99 per cent of our genes are the same as those of a chimpanzee. In fact, chimpanzees are more closely related to humans than they are to gorillas. Like us, the other great apes are intelligent, use tools, solve problems and communicate. They can also learn simple language, although their vocal cords cannot produce enough sounds to speak words.

▼ APE FEATURES
Gorillas are the largest of the great apes. Typical ape features include long arms (longer than their legs), flexible wrist joints, gripping thumbs and fingers, and no tail. Apes are clever, with big brains.

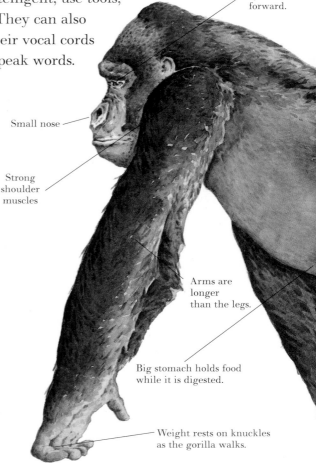

Eyes face forward.

Small nose

Strong shoulder muscles

Arms are longer than the legs.

Big stomach holds food while it is digested.

Weight rests on knuckles as the gorilla walks.

▲ RED APE
Red, shaggy orangutans are the largest tree-living animals in the world. Their name means old-man-of-the-forest. Orangutans live on the islands of Borneo and Sumatra in South-east Asia.

▲ STUDYING APES

Much of what we know today about wild apes is based on the work of scientists such as Dr Dian Fossey, who spent many years carefully observing gorillas in the wild.

GROUPS ▶

Family groups of between five and 40 gorillas live together in the misty rainforests and mountains of central Africa. Each group is led by an adult male. He decides where the group will feed, sleep and travel.

Apes do not have a tail.

King Kong

At the beginning of the 1930s, the film King Kong *showed a giant gorilla as a dangerous monster. In the movie, a team of hunters capture Kong and take him to America. We now know that gorillas are peaceful animals, very different from the movie monster.*

Feet rest flat on the ground.

▼ APE FACES

Have you ever watched a chimpanzee in a zoo and found that it has turned to watch you? Great apes are often as interested in watching us as we are in watching them.

Inside a Great Ape

Characteristic features of great apes
are their long, strong arms and flexible
shoulders, which they use to clamber through
the trees. They do not have tails to help them
balance and grip the branches. Instead of hooves
or paws, apes have hands and feet that can grasp
branches and hold food very well. On the
ground, an ape's strong arms and fingers take its
weight as it walks on all fours. Humans are
different from the other apes as they have short
arms and long legs. Human arms are about
30 per cent shorter than human legs. Our bodies
and bones are also designed for walking upright
rather than for swinging through the trees. All
the apes have a large head, with a big skull
inside, to protect an intelligent brain.

◀ **APE SKELETON**
One of the notable
features of an ape
skeleton is the
large skull that
surrounds and
protects the big
brain. Apes also
have long,
strong finger
and toe bones
for gripping
branches. The
arm bones of
the orangutans,
gorillas and
chimpanzees are also
extended, making
their arms
longer than
their legs.

Did you know? Female orangutans can weigh up to 40kg but males can weigh over 90kg.

▼ **THE BIG FIVE**
All great apes have similar bodies, although a human's body is less
hairy and muscular than the bodies of the other apes. The main
differences between ape bodies lie in the
shape of the skull and also the length of
the arms and legs. Orangutans have
extra-long arms to hang from branches,
while humans have long legs
for walking upright.

Orangutan   Gorilla   Bonobo   Chimpanzee   Human

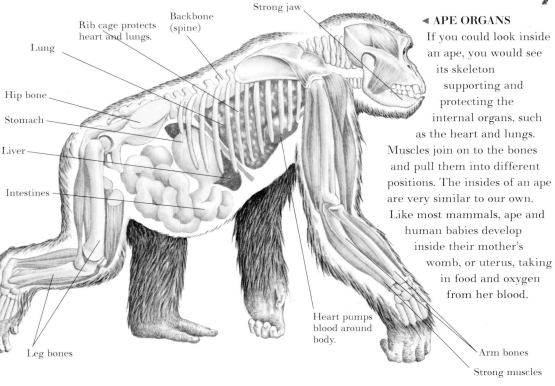

Strong jaw

Backbone
(spine)

Rib cage protects
heart and lungs.

Lung

Hip bone

Stomach

Liver

Intestines

Leg bones

Heart pumps
blood around
body.

Arm bones

Strong muscles

◄ APE ORGANS

If you could look inside
an ape, you would see
its skeleton
supporting and
protecting the
internal organs, such
as the heart and lungs.
Muscles join on to the bones
and pull them into different
positions. The insides of an ape
are very similar to our own.
Like most mammals, ape and
human babies develop
inside their mother's
womb, or uterus, taking
in food and oxygen
from her blood.

▲ NO TAIL

Apes, such as chimpanzees, do not have
tails, but most monkeys do. Apes
clamber and hang by their powerful
arms. Monkeys walk along branches on
all fours, using the tail for balance.

EXTRA HAND ►
Unlike the apes,
monkeys that live
in the dense
rainforests of
Central and South
America have
special gripping
tails, called
prehensile tails.
The tails also have
sensitive tips that
work like an extra
one-fingered
hand, allowing the
apes to cling to
the branches when
gathering fruit.

Wonderful Whales

Whales are mammals and more closely related
to furry land animals than to other fish. Over
many millions of years, whales have
developed features that suit them to a life
spent mostly underwater. They have
long, rounded bodies and smooth,
almost hairless skin. There are
two types of whale: toothed
whales, such as dolphins, feed
on fish, while baleen
whales strain
smaller creatures
from seawater.

▼ BIG MOUTH

This grey whale is a baleen whale. Its baleen –
curtains of fine plates – can be seen hanging
from its upper jaw. The whale filters food from
gulps of seawater by straining it through gaps
between the plates of the baleen.
Baleen whales have large
mouths to take in a
lot of water.

Baleen

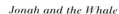

Jonah and the Whale

*This picture from the 17th century tells one of
the best known of all Bible stories. The prophet
Jonah was thrown overboard by sailors during
a terrible storm. To rescue him, God sent a
whale, which swallowed him whole. Jonah
spent three days in the whale's belly before it
coughed him up on to dry land. The picture
shows that many people at this time had little
idea of what a whale looked like. The artist
has given it shark-like teeth and a curly tail.*

▼ LEAPING DOLPHINS

A pair of bottlenose dolphins leap effortlessly several metres out of the water. Powerful muscles near the tail provide them with the energy for fast swimming and leaping. They leap for various reasons – to signal to each other, to look for fish or perhaps just for fun.

LOUSY WHALES ▶

The grey whale's skin is covered with light-coloured patches. These patches are clusters of ten-legged lice, called cyamids, which are 2–3cm long. They feed on the whale's skin.

▲ HANGERS ON

This humpback whale's throat is covered with barnacles, which take hold because the whale moves quite slowly. They cannot easily cling to swifter-moving whales, such as dolphins. A dolphin sheds rough skin as it moves through the water. This also makes it harder for a barnacle to take hold.

◀ BODY LINES

A pod, or group, of melon-headed whales swim in the Pacific Ocean. This species is one of the smaller whales, at less than 3m long. It shows the features of a typical whale – a well-rounded body with a short neck and a single fin on the back. It has a pair of paddle-like front flippers and a tail with horizontal flukes.

Did you know?
Whales have whiskers on their faces.

65

Shark Attack

Sharks are perfect underwater killing machines. All sharks are fish, related to rays and dogfish. Unlike most other fish, sharks do not have bones. Instead their bodies are supported by springy cartilage. Although most sharks are cold-blooded — their bodies are always the same temperature as the seawater — some sharks, such as the great white and mako, can keep their bodies warmer than the water around them. Warm bodies are more efficient, allowing the sharks to swim faster. Sharks have a huge, oil-filled liver that helps to keep them afloat. However, most ocean sharks must swim all the time. If they were to stop, not only would they sink, but they would also be unable to breathe. Some sharks can take a rest on the seabed by pumping water over their gills to breathe.

▲ GILL BREATHERS
Like almost all fish, this sixgill shark breathes by taking oxygen-rich water into its mouth. The oxygen passes through the gills into the blood, and the water leaves through the gill slits.

▲ OCEAN RACER
The shortfin mako shark is the fastest shark in the sea. Using special, warm muscles, it can travel at speeds of 35–50km/h. The sharks use their speed to catch fast-swimming swordfish.

◄ SUSPENDED ANIMATION
The sandtiger shark can hold air in its stomach. The air acts like a life jacket, helping the shark to hover in the water. Sandtiger sharks stay afloat without moving, lurking among rocks and caves as they wait for shoals of fish.

KEEP MOVING ▶
Like many hunting sharks, the grey reef shark cannot breathe unless it moves forward. The forward motion pushes water over its gills. If it stops moving, the shark will drown. Sharks have to swim even when they are asleep.

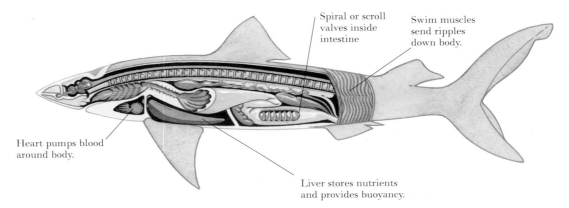

Spiral or scroll valves inside intestine

Swim muscles send ripples down body.

Heart pumps blood around body.

Liver stores nutrients and provides buoyancy.

▲ INSIDE A SHARK
A shark has thick muscles, a spiral or scroll valve in the intestine, which increases the area for absorbing digested food. It also has blood vessels that carry oxygen from the gills around the body.

Did you know? Mako sharks have been seen to leap 6m clear of the water.

◀ ABLE TO REST
The tawny nurse shark pumps water over its gills by lifting the floor of its mouth. This allows it to rest on the seabed, yet still breathe. Whitetip reef sharks, lemon sharks, catsharks and nursehounds also do this.

Animal
Survival

Animals living in the wild are faced with many challenges and they must be constantly aware of their surroundings if they are to survive. The key thing about animals (unlike plants) is that they are able to change their behaviour immediately in response to changes in their environment. In this section we see how they do it ... and survive.

Sensing Survival

If an animal is to survive in the wild, it must be able to find food and water and avoid enemies that might kill and eat it. If it is to ensure the survival of its species, it must also be able to find a mate and produce more creatures of the same kind. All of these activities depend on the senses, with which the animals pick up information about their surroundings.

How the Senses Work

The sense organs, such as the eyes and ears, belong to an animal's nervous system, which is controlled by the brain. Signals from the sense organs travel along nerves to the brain, and the brain decides if any action is necessary. If the animal needs to react, the brain sends signals to the relevant muscles, causing the animal to behave in the correct manner — to hide or to run away from enemies, for example.

Although most animals possess the five basic senses of sight, hearing, smell, taste and touch, they are not equally developed or important. Most birds, for example, have excellent eyesight and a poor sense of smell. Sharks, on the other hand, have poor eyesight and a superb sense of smell. The sense of smell is so important to these fishes that the part of the brain dealing with it is often larger than all the other parts of the brain put together. Many cave-dwelling animals are completely blind and rely largely on the sense of touch to find their way around in the darkness. The sense of touch usually involves various hairs or whiskers that send signals to the brain when

Sharks use smell and sound to find their prey, and can detect water movement, vibrations and electric currents.

disturbed — when they bump into things, for example. The antennae or feelers of many insects are clothed with such hairs.

Some animals rely on very special senses to find their food. Rattlesnakes have heat-sensitive pits on their faces that detect the warmth of their prey. Sharks have special nerves in their noses which mean they can even detect tiny electric currents created by the muscles of their prey.

Eyes and Ears

The eyes of vertebrate animals (those with backbones) all have the
same basic pattern. A lens near the front of the eye gathers light
rays from the surroundings and focuses them on to a retina at
the back. The retina consists of millions of light-sensitive
nerve cells, and when light hits them they send signals
to the brain. These signals are then 'translated' by the
brain into a picture of what the eye is looking at.
Animals that are nocturnal usually have big eyes
because big eyes can collect more light than small ones.
The tarsier and the night monkey, for example, have much
bigger eyes than their day-active relatives. Owls' eyes have
big lenses and are specially constructed to make the best use
of dim light, so the birds can spot prey on the darkest nights.

*Owls have
extremely large eyes
in relation to their body so
they have excellent eyesight.*

Predatory creatures, such as hawks, owls, cats and dogs, usually
have forward-looking eyes. The fields of view of the two eyes overlap
to some extent, providing the binocular vision that enables the animals to judge distances – very
important for animals needing a good aim. Monkeys and apes also have binocular vision, which
enables them to climb and leap safely through the trees. Grazing animals, such as horses, do not
need binocular vision, although some have it to a certain degree. They need all-round vision to
spot approaching predators, so their eyes are usually placed on the sides of the head.

Ears are designed to pick up sounds, which are basically vibrations passing through the air.
Sounds can be warnings, invitations from mates, or the sounds of predators or prey moving
around, and an animal has to be able to distinguish between them. Typically, an ear consists of
a thin membrane linked to nerves. The membrane vibrates like a drumskin when struck by the
vibrating air and sends signals along the nerves to the brain, where the signals are translated.

*A stalking cat must choose the right
moment if it is to catch its prey. A cat's
eyes are set apart at the front of the head,
giving the cat binocular vision, enabling it
to judge the position of its prey exactly.*

Taste and Smell

Known as the chemical senses, taste and smell involve
picking up and identifying different substances in the
surroundings. The sense of taste comes into play when
substances are touched and is concerned mainly with
making sure that things are good to eat. Vertebrates taste
things mainly with their tongues, but insects use their
antennae and also their feet. The sense of smell can detect
food or mates that are several kilometres away by picking
up minute traces of scent in the air or in the water.

Brain Power

Most crucial of all, the brain of an animal must enable it
to interpret the signals received by the senses, and react
correctly to ensure survival.

71

Insect Senses

Most insects have keen senses, but they do not sense the world in the same way that humans do. The main sense organs are on the head, but many types of insects use other parts of their body to tell them about their surroundings. For example, many crickets have ears on their forelegs, while flies taste their food with their hairy feet.

Insect eyes are very different from our own. Most insects have compound eyes, which are made up of many tiny lenses. These are particularly good at sensing movement, but cannot make sharp images. Several insects, such as fleas and some beetles and bugs, have very simple eyes that only detect light or dark.

An insect's antennae are its main sense tools. Most are used for smelling and feeling, and in some species for hearing and tasting, too. Sensitive hairs all over the insects' bodies pick up tiny currents in the air, which may alert them to nearby enemies.

◀ **SPINY SENSORS**

Tanner beetles have long, curving antennae that are very sensitive feelers. The antennae are covered with tiny hairs. Each hair is attached to a nerve that alerts the insect's brain when the hair touches an object or is moved by air currents.

▲ **BRANCHING ANTENNAE**

This unusual beetle from Central America has branched antennae that look like the antlers of a stag. The branches are usually held closed, but the insect can fan them out to detect chemicals carried on the wind, such as the scent of a faraway mate. Smells such as these would be far too faint for humans to detect.

SMELL AND TOUCH ▶

Longhorn beetles are named for their long antennae. Some kinds have antennae that are twice as long as their bodies. An insect's antennae are sometimes called its 'feelers'. The term is rather misleading – the antennae are used for feeling, but their main function is to pick up scents.

◀ ELBOW-SHAPED
The weevil's antennae are attached to its long snout. Many weevils have jointed antennae, which bend in the middle like a human arm at the elbow. Some have special organs at the base of their antennae, which vibrate to sound and act as ears. This brush-snouted weevil has a bushy 'beard' of long, sensitive hairs on its snout.

COMPOUND EYES ▶
The huge eyes of the harlequin beetle cover the front of its head. Only the area from which its antennae sprout remains uncovered. Each compound eye is made up of hundreds of tiny lenses, each one of which works in the same way as a human eye. Scientists believe that the signals from each lens build up to create one large picture.

◀ TINY LENSES
A close-up of a beetle's compound eye shows that it is made up of many tiny facets, each of which points in a slightly different direction. Each is made up of a lens at the surface and a second lens inside. The lenses focus light down a central structure inside the eye, called the rhabdome, on to a bundle of nerve fibres, which are behind the eye. The nerve fibres then send messages to the brain. The hundreds of tiny lenses probably do not create the detailed, focused image produced by the human eye. However, they can pick up colours and shapes and are very good at detecting tiny movements.

Focus on

KEEPING WARM

Butterflies and moths can only fly if their body temperature reaches at least 25–30°C. If they are too cold, the muscles powering the wings do not work well enough. To warm up, butterflies bask in the sun, so that the wing scales soak up heat like solar panels. Night-flying moths shiver their wings to warm them instead.

Most adult insects have one or two pairs of wings. They fly by simply beating their wings very rapidly to move through the air. This sort of flight takes a lot of energy and can only be used for short journeys. Butterflies and moths, however, fly in a different way that is closer to birds' flight than that of other insects. They save energy by rippling their wings slowly up and down. Some, such as the white admiral, can even glide on currents of air with just an occasional flap to keep them aloft. This enables them to fly amazing distances. Smaller moths and butterflies beat their wings faster than larger species (kinds). Skipper butterflies have the fastest wingbeats of all. Hawk moths are the fastest-flying insects. Their narrow wings beat rapidly to keep them aloft. Birdwing butterflies have the largest wings, which can be 30cm across.

WING TIPS

To the human eye, the wings of butterflies and moths appear simply to flap. However, freeze-frame photography reveals that the bases of the wings twist as they move up and down, so that the wing tips move in a figure of eight.

DODGING DANGER

Butterflies look like clumsy fliers, but their acrobatic twists and turns enable them to escape sparrows and other predatory birds. Some moths can fly at up to 48km/h when frightened.

74

Flight

The wings push air backwards.

The butterfly is propelled forwards.

A butterfly lifts its wings upwards.

As the wings come down again, they provide lift to keep the butterfly up.

WING FLEXIBILITY

The base and front edge of each wing is stiff, but the rest of the wing is flexible. The stiff front edge of the wing produces a lifting force, like the wings of an aircraft, as it flies through the air. The bending of the rest of the wing pushes air backwards and drives the butterfly forwards.

FANCY FLIERS

Butterflies such as this painted lady are very efficient fliers. They tend to flap their wings only occasionally when in flight. They prefer to glide gracefully from flower to flower, with just the odd beat of their wings.

Spider Senses

Most spiders have poor eyesight and rely mainly on scents and vibrations to give them information about their surroundings. Even spiders with good eyesight, such as the jumping spiders, can see only up to 30cm away. Most spiders have eight eyes arranged in two or three rows. The eyes are pearly or dark and are usually protected by several bristles. Spider eyes are called ocelli and are of two types. Main eyes produce a focused image and help in judging distances. Secondary eyes are smaller and have light-sensitive cells to pick up motion.

▲ **NO EYES**
This cave spider has no need for eyes, because there is no light in the cave for the spider to see. Like many animals that live in the dark it relies on other senses. It especially uses many sensitive hairs to find its way around, taste its prey and sense the movements of its enemies.

◄ **BIG EYES**
A spider's main eyes are always the middle pair of eyes in the front row. In most spiders even the main eyes are small, but this jumping spider has very well developed main eyes, as this enlarged picture shows. They work rather like a telephoto lens on a camera. Inside, the large lens focuses light on to four layers of sensitive cells. The main eyes see clearly over a small area a few centimetres away and let the spider stalk and pounce when it gets close to its prey.

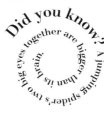
Did you know? A jumping spider's two big eyes together are bigger than its brain.

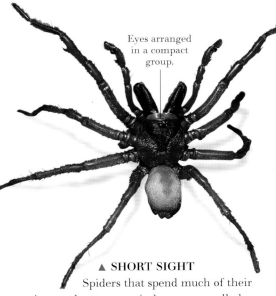

Eyes arranged in a compact group.

▲ HUNTSMAN SPIDER

The giant huntsman is an agile, night-time hunter. Most hunting spiders have fairly large front eyes to help them find and pounce on prey in the dark. Secondary eyes help the hunters see in three dimensions over a wider area. They detect changes in light and dark.

▲ SHORT SIGHT

Spiders that spend much of their time under stones or in burrows usually have small eyes. This trapdoor spider has eight tiny eyes in a close group. Spiders that catch their prey in webs also have very poor eyesight. These spiders rely much more on their sense of touch than their eyesight. They use their legs to taste objects around them.

A large-eyed wolf spider

The small eyes of an orb-weaver

A six-eyed woodlouse spider

A jumping spider

▲ EYES FOR HUNTING

The spiders with the best eyesight are active daylight hunters such as this jumping spider. A jumping spider's eight eyes are arranged in three rows with four in the front, two in the middle and two at the back of the head. Lynx spiders and wolf spiders also have good eyesight.

▲ ALL KINDS OF EYES

The position and arrangement of a spider's eyes can help us to determine what type of spider it is and how it catches food. A small number of spiders only have six eyes or fewer. Many male money spiders have eyes on top of little lobes or turrets sticking up from the head.

Crawling Creatures

Have you ever seen a spider scuttle swiftly away?
Spiders sometimes move quickly, but cannot keep
going for long. Their breathing system is not very
efficient, so they soon run out of puff.

Spiders can walk, run, jump, climb and hang
upside down. Each spider's leg has seven sections.
The legs are moved by sets of muscles and by
pumping blood into them. At the end of each
leg are two or three sharp claws for
gripping surfaces. Spiders that spin webs cling to
strands of silk with their claws. Hunting spiders
have dense tufts of hair between the claws for
gripping smooth surfaces and for holding prey.

▲ **AERONAUT**
Many young or
small spiders drift
through the air on
strands of silk. Spiders
carried away on warm air
currents use this method
to find new places to live.

▲ **WATER WALKER**
The fishing spider is also called the raft or swamp spider. It
stands on the surface skin of water. Its long legs spread its weight
over the surface so it does not fall through. Little dips form in
the stretchy skin of the water around each leg tip.

▲ **SAFETY LINE**
This garden spider is
climbing up a silk dragline.
Spiders drop down these lines
if they are disturbed. They
pay out the line as they go,
moving very quickly. As they
fall, spiders pull in their legs,
making them harder to see.

78

▲ SPIDER LEGS

Muscles in the legs of this trapdoor spider bend the joints rather like we bend our knees. To stretch out the legs, however, the spider has to pump blood into them. If a spider is hurt and blood leaks out, it cannot escape from enemies.

▲ CHAMPION JUMPERS

Jumping spiders are champions of the long jump. They secure themselves with a safety line before they leap. Some species can leap more than 40 times the length of their own bodies.

▼ CLAWED FEET

Two toothed claws on the ends of a spider's feet enable it to grip surfaces as it walks. Web-building spiders have a third, middle claw that hooks over the silk lines of the web and holds the silk against barbed hairs. This allows the spider to grip the smooth, dry silk of its web without falling or slipping.

Scopulate pad

Toothed claw

Middle hook

Barbed hair

▲ HAIRY FEET

Many hunting spiders have dense tufts of short hairs called scopulae between the claws. The end of each hair is split into many tiny hairs a bit like a brush. These hairs pull up some of the moisture coating most surfaces, gluing the spider's leg down. Spiders with these feet can climb up smooth surfaces such as glass.

79

▲ EYESIGHT
Snakes have no eyelids to cover their eyes. The snakes with the best eyesight are tree snakes, such as this green mamba.

Snake Senses

To find prey and avoid enemies, snakes rely more on their senses of smell, taste and touch than on sight and hearing. Snakes have no eardrums, so cannot hear sounds in the normal way. But their jawbones pick up sound vibrations travelling through the ground and pass them to a bone connected to the inner ear. As well as ordinary senses, snakes also have some special ones. They are among the few animals that smell with their tongues.

▲ NIGHT HUNTER
The horned viper's eyes open wide at night (*above*). During the day, its pupils close to narrow slits (*below*).

Heat pits

▲ SENSING HEAT
The green tree python has heat-sensitive pits on its face that pick up the warmth of its prey.

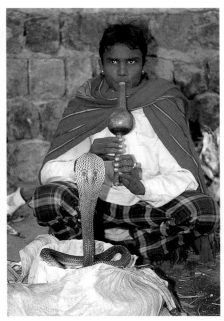

◄ **THE FORKED TONGUE**
This black-tailed rattlesnake is flicking its tongue to taste the air. The forked tongue picks up tiny chemical particles of scent.

▲ **HEARING**
As it has no ears, the cobra cannot hear the music played by the snake charmer. It follows the movements of the pipe, which resembles a snake, and rises up as it prepares to defend itself.

► **JACOBSON'S ORGAN**
As a snake draws its tongue back into its mouth, it presses the forked tip into the two openings of the Jacobson's organ. This organ is in the roof of the mouth and it identifies scents picked up by the tongue.

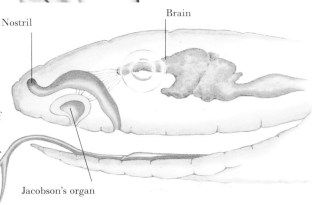

Nostril

Brain

Jacobson's organ

Slither and Slide

For animals without legs, snakes move around very well. They can glide over or under the ground, climb trees and swim through water. A few snakes can even parachute through the air. Snakes are not speedy – most move at about 3km/h. With their bendy backbones, snakes wriggle their bodies in the shape of a wave. They push themselves along using muscles joined to their ribs. The scales on their skin also grip the ground to help with movement.

Did you know? A person can walk faster than most snakes can move

Corn snake
(Elaphe guttata)

► **S-SHAPED MOVER**
Most snakes move in an S-shaped path, pushing the side curves of their bodies backwards against the surface they are travelling on or through. The muscular waves of the snake's body push against surrounding objects and the body is pushed forward.

▼ **SKINNY SNAKE**
The green whip snake lives in the flimsy branches of forest trees. It curves its thin body into wide loops that spread the snake's weight over several branches.

▲ **SWIMMING SNAKE**
The banded sea snake's stripes stand out as it glides through the water. Snakes swim using S-shaped movements. A sea snake's tail is flattened from side to side to give it extra power, like the oar of a rowing boat.

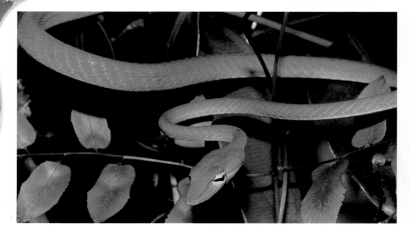

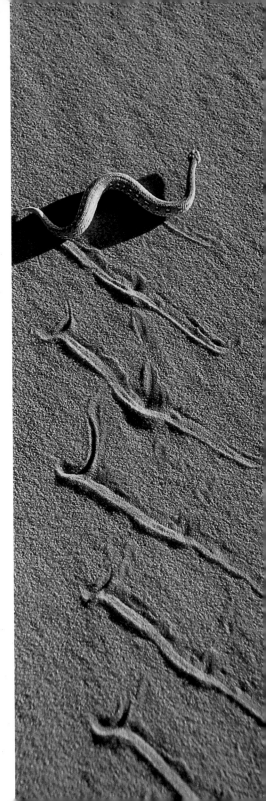

▶ SIDEWINDING

The way snakes that live on loose sand move along is called sidewinding. The snake anchors its head and tail in the sand and throws the middle part of its body sideways.

Did you know? The fastest land snake is the black mamba, moving at up to 11 km/h.

▼ HOW SNAKES MOVE

Most land snakes move in four different ways, depending on the type of ground they are crossing and the type of snake.

1 S-shaped movement: the snake wriggles from side to side.

2 Concertina movement: the snake pulls one half of its body along first, then the other half.

3 Sidewinding movement: the snake throws the middle part of its body sideways, keeping the head and tail on the ground.

4 Caterpillar movement: the snake uses its belly scales to pull itself along in a straight line.

Crocodilian Senses

The senses of sight, hearing, smell, taste and touch are much more powerful in a crocodilian than in other living reptiles. They have good eyesight and can see in colour. Their eyes are also adapted to seeing well in the dark, which is useful because they hunt mainly at night. Crocodilians also have sharp hearing. They sense the sounds of danger or prey moving nearby and listen for the barks, coughs and roars of their own species at mating time. Crocodilians also have sensitive scales along the sides of their jaws, which help to feel and capture prey underwater.

▲ NOISY GATORS
An American alligator bellows loudly to attract mates. Noises such as hissing or snarling are made at enemies. Young alligators call for help from adults. Small ear slits behind the eyes are kept open when the animal is out of the water. Flaps close to protect the ears when the animal submerges.

Did you know? Crocodiles shake their ear flaps up and down when they are angry.

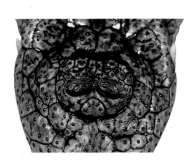

▲ SMELL DETECTORS
A Nile crocodile picks up chemical signals through the nostrils at the tip of its snout. These smelly messages help it to detect prey and others of its kind. Crocodiles can smell food over long distances. They are known to have come from as far away as 3km to feed together on the carcass of a large animal.

Crocodile Tears
According to legend, crocodiles cry to make people feel so sorry for them that they come near enough for the crocodiles to catch them. Crocodiles are also supposed to shed tears of remorse before finishing their meal. It is said that people cry crocodile tears when they seem to be sorry for something, but really are not. Real-life crocodiles cannot cry but sometimes look as if they are.

▶ TASTY TONGUE

Inside the gaping mouth of this American crocodile is a wide, fleshy tongue. It is joined to the bottom of the mouth and does not move, so it plays no part in catching prey. We know that crocodilians have taste buds lining their mouths because some prefer one type of food to another. They can tell the difference between sweet and sour tastes. They also have salt glands on their tongues that get rid of excess salt. Salt builds up in the body over time if the animal lives in the sea or a very dry environment.

◀ GLOW-IN-THE-DARK EYES

A torch shone into a crocodile farm at night makes the dark glow eerily with a thousand living lights. The scientific explanation is that a special layer at the back of the eye reflects light back into the front of the eye. This makes sure that the eye catches as much light as possible. Above water, crocodilians see well and are able to spot prey up to 90m away. Underwater, an inner, transparent lid covers the eye. This makes their eyesight foggy, rather like looking through thick goggles.

▶ A PREDATOR'S EYE

The eye of a spectacled caiman, like all crocodilians, has both upper and lower lids. A third eyelid at the side, called a nictitating (blinking) membrane, moves across to clean the eye's surface. The dark, vertical pupil narrows to a slit to stop bright light damaging the inside. At night, the pupil opens wide to let any available light into the eye. A round pupil, such as a human's, cannot open as wide.

Land and Water

Have you ever seen a film of an alligator gliding through the water with slow, S-shaped sweeps of its powerful tail? Crocodilians move gracefully and easily in the water. They use very little energy to do this and keep most of their body hidden under the surface. Their legs lie close alongside their body to make them streamlined and to cut down drag from the water. Legs may also be used as rudders to change course. With their short legs, crocodilians appear to lumber along clumsily on land, dragging their tail behind them. However, they can move fast if they need to. Some can gallop at 17km/h when running over short distances of up to 100m. Crocodilians also sometimes drag themselves along in what is called a belly slide. With side-to-side twists of the body, the animal uses its legs to push along on its belly. This tobogganing movement is used to slip quietly into the water.

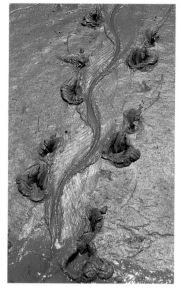

▲ BEST FOOT FORWARD
The tracks of a saltwater crocodile in the mud show how its legs move in sequence. The right front leg goes forward first, then the back left leg. The front left leg goes forward next, and finally the right back leg moves. The tail snakes along the ground between the footprints.

▼ THE HIGH WALK
To move on land, crocodilians hold their legs underneath their body, lifting most of the tail off the ground. This is called the high walk. It is very different from the walk of a lizard, which keeps its legs sprawled out at the sides of its body. The tail is dragged behind the body in the high walk, but if the animal starts to run, the tail swings from side to side. A special ankle joint lets crocodilians twist and turn their legs in the high walk.

▲ FLOATING AROUND

This Nile crocodile is floating near the surface of Lake Tanganyika, Tanzania, Africa. It is holding its feet out to the sides for balance. The toes and the webbing between them are spread out for extra stability. When the crocodile floats, its tail hangs down, but when it swims its body becomes horizontal.

► TAIL WALKING

Some crocodilians can leap straight up out of the water. They seem to be walking on their tails in the same way that a dolphin can travel backwards on its strong tail. This movement is, however, unusual. Large crocodiles will also spring upwards, propelled by their back legs, to grab prey unawares.

► FEET AND TOES

On the front feet, crocodilians have five separate digits (toes). These sometimes have webbing (skin) stretched between them. The back feet are always webbed to help them balance and move in the water. There are only four toes on the back feet. The fifth toe is just a small bone inside the foot.

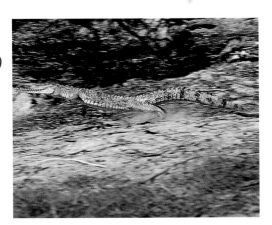

▲ THE GALLOP

The fastest way for a crocodilian to move on land is to gallop. Only a few crocodilians, such as the Johnston's crocodile shown above, make a habit of moving like this. In a gallop, the back legs push the crocodilian forward in a leap, and the front legs stretch out to catch the body as it lands at the end of the leap. Then the back legs swing forward to push the animal forward again.

Eagle Eyes and Ears

Humans rely on five senses to find out about the world. They are sight, hearing, smell, taste and touch. However, most birds use just the two senses of sight and hearing. In birds of prey, sight is by far the most important sense for finding and hunting the prey they need to survive. Their eyes are exceptionally large in relation to the size of their head, and they are set in the skull so that they look forwards. This binocular (two-eyed) forward vision enables them to judge distances accurately when hunting. Owls have particularly large eyes that are well adapted for seeing in dim light. These birds are equally dependent on hearing to find prey in the dark. Some harriers and hawks use their keen sense of hearing to hunt, too. Birds' ear openings are quite small. They are set back from the eyes and cannot be seen because they are covered in feathers.

Common buzzard (*Buteo buteo*)

▲ OPEN WIDE

A common buzzard opens its beak wide to make its distinctive mewing call. This bird has extremely large eyes in relation to its body, so it has excellent eyesight. The forward-facing eyes give it good stereoscopic (3D) vision and the ability to pinpoint the exact position of a mouse in the grass 100m away.

◄ NOT TO BE SNIFFED AT

The turkey vulture of North and South America, like all New World vultures, has nostrils that you can see right through. Its nose is very sensitive. This enables the turkey vulture to sniff out dead animals on the ground while it is flying high above the forest.

Turkey vulture (*Cathartes aura*)

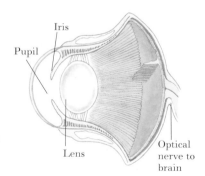

Iris

Pupil

Lens

Optical nerve to brain

▲ OWL EYE

The owl has exceptional eyesight. Its unusual eye-shape, with a large lens, enables it to form a clear image even on a dark night.

Spotted eagle owl (*Bubo africanus*)

◄ FORWARD FACE

The African spotted eagle owl has big eyes.
The pupil (centre) and lens are especially
large to allow more light to enter and provide
the owl with good night vision. The eyes are
set in a flat facial disc. The earlike projections
on top of the owl's head are actually
ornamental tufts of feathers used for display.
The true ears are hidden under stiff feathers
at either side of the facial disc. The disc
collects sounds like a satellite dish,
directing them to the sensitive ears.

► ON THE LOOKOUT

This large falcon, called a
lanner, is soaring high in the
sky on outstretched wings,
looking down with its sharp
eyes on the scene below. If the
lanner sees a flying bird, it will
fold back its wings and dive on
the unsuspecting bird. The
lanner will hit the bird at high
speed and usually break the
bird's neck. Then it will either
snatch the bird in mid-air or
pick it up off the ground.

◄ MONTAGU'S EYEBROW

The Montagu's harrier is a slender,
long-legged hawk with an
owl-like facial ruff. The eyes
are surrounded by a small
bony ridge covered in feathers,
called a supraorbital ridge. It
probably helps protect the
harrier's eyes from attack when
the bird goes hunting, and may
also act as a shield against the
sun's rays when it is flying.

Montagu's harrier
(*Circus pygargus*)

On the Wing

The wings of all birds work in the same way. Strong pectoral (chest) muscles make the wings flap and drive the bird through the air. As they move through the air, the wings produce a lift force, which supports the bird's weight. All birds have differently shaped wings that are adapted to their way of life. Large birds of prey (raptors), such as vultures, spend much of their time soaring high in the sky. These birds have long, broad wings that enable them to glide on air currents. The smaller hawks, such as the sparrowhawk, have short, rounded wings and a long tail for rapid, darting flight through woodland. A bird's tail is also important for flying. It acts much like a ship's rudder, steadying the bird's body and guiding it through the air. It can be fanned out to give extra lift and also helps the bird to slow down.

▲ WING FINGERS
An African fish eagle takes to the air. Like other eagles, it has broad wings and fingered wing tips, seen plainly here. The 'fingers' reduce air turbulence around the wings, giving better lift.

Mauritius kestrel
(*Falco punctatus*)

◄ AGILE BIRD
The Mauritius kestrel has a broad tail and, for a raptor, fairly short wings. These two features help it to manoeuvre well in the woodland habitat in which it lives. It lives on the island of Mauritius, in the Indian Ocean.

▲ DROPPING IN
A sparrowhawk's large tail enables it to twist and turn effortlessly in and out of cover as it hunts for prey. This sparrowhawk's wings beat rapidly and provide enough speed for it to surprise its unsuspecting prey.

Eagle of the Gods

In Greek mythology, the eagle was the favoured bird of the mighty Zeus. Zeus was god of the sky, lord of the winds and rains, and king among the gods. He is often depicted holding a thunderbolt in his right hand, with an eagle standing at his feet. Here we see him riding in a chariot, drawn by a pair of his sacred birds.

▼ LIKE AN ARROW

The sharply pointed wings tell us that this bird is a falcon. In fact, it is a lanner falcon. A bird can fly extremely fast with pointed wings because the wings cut through the air and offer little wind resistance. Lanner falcons hunt over open ground and use pure speed to catch slower-flying birds.

Lanner falcon (*Falco biarmicus*)

▲ BUILT TO SOAR

A white-backed vulture soars high in the sky with its broad wings fully outstretched, on the lookout for carcasses on the ground. Using air currents, a vulture can remain in the air for a long time, because its wings provide plenty of lift.

► READY, STEADY, GO

A young male kestrel takes off in a multiple-exposure photograph. First the bird thrusts its body forwards and raises its wings. Its wings extend and beat downwards, pushing slightly backwards. As the air is forced back, the bird is driven forwards. At the same time, air moving over the wings gives the bird the lift it needs to keep itself airborne.

Sensing the World

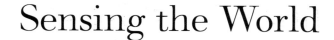

Horses have relatively large brains that interpret information from their well-developed senses. As a result, horses and their relatives have excellent memories, a brilliant sense of direction and an extraordinary ability to sense danger. The senses work together in other ways, too. Eyes are set well back on each side of the skull, giving almost all-round vision. But there is a blind spot directly behind the head. To cover this, the horse swivels its ears right around and uses its sense of hearing to check behind itself. When both the horse's eyes look straight ahead they operate together to produce clear three-dimensional images. This enables horses to judge distances well, which is important when they are jumping obstacles.

▲ CHECK IT OUT

A stallion (male horse) uses its good sense of smell to investigate piles of dung and urine from another herd. He will find out how recently the other herd passed by, if it contains a mare (female) ready to mate and if the herd is led by another stallion.

GATHERING SMELLS ▶

Curling back its lips in this way is a horse's reaction to unfamiliar smells. It is known as the flehmen reaction and is also used to find mares that are ready to breed. With its acute sense of smell, a horse can be alerted to predators and sniff out fresh grass and water.

▲ THE TASTE TEST

Little is known about a horse's sense of taste, although it is likely to be fairly sensitive. This can be seen from the way it grazes, pushing aside some plants to reach others. Taste may also be involved when horses groom each other.

▲ CLEVER HORSE

Memory is important for survival. Remembering where water or food can be found and which plants are good to eat may be a matter of life or death for a wild horse. Horses do well in intelligence and memory tests. In one test, horses were taught to recognize patterns. When they were tested a year later they could remember almost all of them, scoring better than most humans would.

▼ SHARP EYES

A horse can see objects clearly at short and long distances at the same time because images form on different areas of the eye. This is useful for keeping watch for predators while grazing. (Human eyes have variable focus that automatically adjusts to distances.) A horse can see better than a cat or a dog during daylight, and its night-time vision is also very good.

◄ ALERT EARS

All horses have ears that behave rather like radar dishes. They can turn in the direction of a sound quite independently of each other, while the rest of the body remains still. The rotating action is operated by no fewer than 16 muscles. This, together with the large size of the outer ear, means that a horse's sense of hearing is far more acute than a human's.

Running Like the Wind

▲ **THE TROT**

Once a horse reaches a certain walking speed, it becomes more energy-efficient to trot. In order to go faster, the feet leave the ground to incorporate little springs forward into the movement. Top trotting speed is about 14km/h for the average horse.

The way in which a horse moves makes the most of its energy reserves. The main thrust comes from the hind legs. The forelegs cushion jolts during running and jumping. Horses, zebras and donkeys (equids) have four ways of moving – walking, trotting, cantering and galloping. Each is designed to conserve energy at different speeds.

The hooves of wild and domestic horses are broad. This spreads weight over a wide area so that the hoof does not dig into the ground. Equids that live in rocky or mountainous areas, such as the Asiatic wild horse and the mountain zebra, have narrower hooves that are better for crossing rough ground.

▲ **THE CANTER**

A cantering horse has a rocking action and moves at 15–20km/h. The legs move one after the other, making a smoother action than the trot. Horses canter to cover distances quickly, perhaps when moving to a waterhole.

▲ **THE GALLOP**

The gallop is a horse's fastest way of moving, used when escaping predators. Horses and asses can gallop up to speeds of 50km/h. The gallop is designed for stability and best use of energy. The animal stretches its limbs to their limits, making a smooth action that reduces the shock of hitting the ground at speed.

► SWIMMING
A herd of semi-wild horses in Portugal wades and swims across a wide river. All equids can swim. Even foals can swim from very early days, though they keep close to protective mares.

◄ NURSERY NAP
A foal rests on its side with its limbs extended. Foals lie down more frequently than adults. Horses usually rest standing up as their heart and lungs have to work harder when they are lying down.

▼ BEDTIME
This herd of Przewalski's horses is fast asleep. In any 24-hour period, a horse is alert for about 19 hours, drowsy for two and asleep for three. Sleep is taken in short bursts. Horses do not sleep for long periods as they need to be alert to predators.

Rakahsh
The legendary Persian hero Rustam had a horse called Rakahsh, who was renowned for his speed and strength. Their adventures are told in the Book of Kings, *an 11th-century epic poem. Among many stories of the horse's bravery is the tale of a lion attacking the Persian camp. Rakahsh killed the lion and saved the day.*

95

Elephant Senses

Elephants use the five senses to learn about their surroundings — hearing, sight, smell, touch and taste. The most important sense is smell, which they rely on more than any other. Elephants smell through the trunk, using it as a directional nose. The trunk is also particularly sensitive to touch and has short hairs that help the elephant feel things. The tip of the trunk is used to investigate food, water and other objects. It can tell whether something is hot, cold, sharp or smooth. Elephants communicate with each other largely by sound. They make rumbling sounds, most of which are too low for humans to hear. Touch is also crucial for communication. When two elephants meet, each places the tip of its trunk in the other's mouth as a greeting.

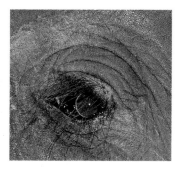

▲ **ELEPHANT EYES**
All elephants' eyes are brown with long lashes. They are small in relation to the huge head. Elephants are colour blind and do not see well in direct, strong sunlight. Their eyesight is better in darker, forest conditions.

Did you know? An African elephant's ear is as big as a single bed sheet and can weigh as much as a person.

◄ **SMELL**
An elephant raises its trunk like a periscope at the slightest scent of danger. It can tell who or what is coming towards it just from the smells picked up by the sensitive trunk. The sense of smell is so powerful that an elephant can pick up the scent of a human being from more than 1.5km away.

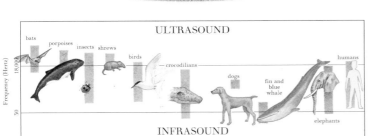

ULTRASOUND

Frequency (Hertz)

18,000

30

INFRASOUND

bats
porpoises
insects shrews
birds
crocodilians
dogs
fin and blue whale
humans
elephants

◀ USING EARS

An elephant strains to hear a distant noise by putting its ears forward to catch the sound. It also does this when it is curious about a certain noise. Elephants have a well-developed sense of hearing. Their enormous ears can pick up the rumble of other elephants up to about 8km away. Male elephants also flap their ears to spread a special scent that lets other elephants know they are there.

◀ HEARING RANGE

Elephants can hear low sounds called infrasound. Human beings cannot hear infrasound although we can sometimes feel it. Some animals, such as bats and mice, can hear very high sounds called ultrasound.

▲ SENSE OF TOUCH

A young elephant is touched by its mother or another close relative every few seconds. This constant reassurance keeps it from being frightened. Elephants also touch each other when they meet. They often stand resting with their bodies touching.

▲ QUICK LEARNERS

Some young working elephants learn to stop their bells ringing by pushing mud inside them. This allows the clever animals to steal food from farmers' fields without being heard.

On the Move

An elephant looks like a noisy, clumsy animal. In fact, it moves about quietly and is surprisingly agile. Forest elephants can quickly disappear into the trees like silent, grey ghosts. The secret of the elephant's silent movement is the way its foot is made. A fatty pad inside the foot cushions the impact of the foot on the ground. The sole then spreads out to take the weight of each step. Elephants usually walk slowly, at a rate of about 6km/h. They can run at more than 40km/h when angry or frightened, but only for a short distance. Elephants swim well, too, and they often reach islands in lakes or off the coast. Ridged soles grip the ground well and enable the animals to climb steep slopes. However, elephants cannot jump. They would crush their legs on impact.

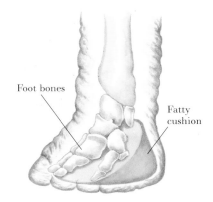

Foot bones

Fatty cushion

▲ FATTY FOOT

An elephant's enormous weight rests on the tips of its toes and on a fatty cushion that works like a giant shock absorber. This shock absorber spreads out as the elephant puts its foot down and contracts as the foot is lifted off the ground. On firm ground, the elephant leaves only faint footprints.

Did you know? An elephant's foot measures up to 1.5m around.

◄ ELEPHANT WALK
An elephant walks and runs with shuffling steps. It cannot trot, canter or gallop. Occasionally, elephants walk backwards. They sometimes find this easier than turning around, which can be a difficult manoeuvre for an elephant.

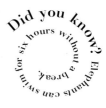

◄ GRIPPING SOLES

The skin on the sole of an elephant's foot is thick and covered in cracks and deep ridges. These help it to grip the ground effectively, rather like the treads on tyres or hiking boots.

Did you know? *Elephants can swim for six hours without a break.*

Royal Hunts
An Indian mythical story tells of King Khusraw, who was killed by his son Shirvieh. In the scene shown here, Shirvieh travels by elephant to the Royal Palace. Here he becomes caught up in a royal hunt. In India, people often rode elephants to hunt.

◄ FOOTCARE

An elephant has a thorn removed from its foot. Elephants in captivity move about less than they do in the wild. As a result, their feet are less tough and need to be looked after. Toenails are not worn away either, so they have to be trimmed.

► ON THE MARCH

A line of elephants crosses the savanna in Kenya. They sometimes march along with each elephant holding the tail of the one in front. They usually walk about 25km a day, but in the hot deserts of Namibia in southwest Africa they have been known to walk up to 195km a day in search of water.

99

Bear Brain and Senses

All bears are very intelligent. Size for size, they have larger brains than dogs and cats. They can remember sources of food and are very curious. Bears use their brains to find food or a mate, and to stay out of trouble. Although closely related to the meat-eating mammals (carnivores) most bears are mainly plant-eaters, so they have no need of hunting tactics. They rely on smell to find their food and the part of the brain that analyses scent is larger than in any of the meat-eaters. Their eyes and ears are small compared to their head size. Bears cannot see distant objects very clearly, but they have colour vision to recognize edible fruits and nuts. Bears often do not see or hear people approaching and may attack in self-defence.

▼ SCENT MARKING
An American black bear cub practises marking a tree by scratching. When it is older, the bear will leave a scent mark to indicate to other bears that the territory is occupied.

◄ TEMPER TANTRUM
A threatened brown bear puts on a fierce display. First it beats the ground or vegetation with its front feet. Then it stands up on its back legs to look larger. This is accompanied by a high-pitched snorting through open lips or a series of hoarse barks. The display of aggression finishes with snapping the jaws together.

▲ FOLLOW YOUR NOSE

A brown bear relies more on smell than sight. It often raises its head and sniffs the air to check out who or what is about. It can detect the faintest trace of a smell, searching for others of its kind.

▼ GETTING TO KNOW YOU

Polar bear cubs rub against their mother to spread her scent over themselves. Smell allows a mother and cubs to recognize each other. They also communicate with sounds. Distressed cubs make low-pitched snores that develop into high whines.

Bruno the Bear

Aesop's Fables are a set of tales written by the ancient Greek writer Aesop. One fable features Bruno the Bear. He is shown as stupid and easily deceived. Bears were considered slow-witted because they sleep a lot. But Bruno was kind, unlike the cunning Reynard the Fox. Bruno cared about others and forgave those who played pranks on him. Bruno was the forerunner of characters such as Winnie-the-Pooh.

▲ SNOWY SCENT TRAIL

Even in the Arctic, polar bears can pick up the trails of other bears and follow them. There are few objects around to use as scent posts for polar bears, so trails may be marked with dribbles of smelly urine.

Tree Climbers

Trees provide food for some bears and a place
of safety for others. Sun bears, sloth bears
and spectacled bears climb trees regularly in
search of food, such as fruits, seeds and nuts,
as well as birds' eggs. Black bears are also
agile tree-climbers. Polar bears very rarely
encounter trees, although a few come into
forested areas during the summer, where
they rest in hollows dug among tree roots to
avoid the heat. Brown bear cubs climb trees
to escape danger, but adult brown bears are
too heavy to be good climbers. A female sloth
bear will carry her small cubs into a tree on
her back, unless she is escaping from a leopard
since they can also climb trees! Most bears
also use trees to mark their
territory. They scratch
the bark and rub on
scents to tell other
bears they are there.

◀ TREE-TOP HOME
The sun bear seeks out
the nests of termites
and bees, and will rip
away bark to get at insects
hidden underneath.
Although the sun bear feeds
mainly on insects it also eats
ripe fruit and preys on small
rodents, birds and lizards.

▶ BEAR DANGER
A mother American
black bear sends her
cubs up into a tree
while she stands
guard at its base.
If the danger is from
an adult brown bear,
the female will flee
and return later for
her cubs when
the bear
has gone.

▲ BELOW THE BARK
An adult, cinnamon-coloured Asian
black bear is able to climb into a
tree with ease using its short but
sturdy claws. It can also lift bark to
lick out insects with a long tongue.

▲ UP A TREE

Giant pandas stay mainly on the ground, but they climb
trees occasionally. They do so to sun themselves or to rest.
Female pandas sometimes head up a tree to escape males,
while males climb trees to advertise their presence.

▼ SAFE HAVEN

Black bears are normally found in
forested areas. They have favourite
trees located along trails where
bears and other animals regularly
pass. The bear marks the tree with
its scent and climbs into the branches
where it
is safe
from larger
brown
bears.

Short, sturdy claws
on a black bear's
feet make tree
climbing easy.

▼ TREE HOUSE

Spectacled bears pull branches together to make a
feeding platform. From here the bears feed on mainly
tough plants called bromeliads. They also eat fruits,
nuts and honey, and may take mice,
forest rabbits and insects on
to the platform
to eat.

▲ HIGH SCHOOL

Black bear cubs stay close to their mother
both on the ground and in a tree. They
watch and learn from her how to climb
and find food among the branches.

Watching Out

To hunt well and not be seen or heard by prey or enemies, cats use their senses of sight and hearing. Cats' eyesight is excellent. Their eyes are adapted for night vision, but they can also see well in the day. Cats' eyes are big compared to the size of their heads. Their eyes work as a pair (binocular vision), which allows cats to accurately judge how far away objects are. At night, cats see in black and white. They can see colours in the day, but not as well as humans can. Cats have very good hearing, much better than a human's. They can hear small animals rustling through the grass or even moving around in their burrows underground.

Did you know? A cat's pupils open wide when it is frightened and close up when it is angry.

▲ CAUGHT IN BRIGHT LIGHT
Cats' eyes are very sensitive to light. During the day in bright light, the pupils of the eyes close right down, letting in only as much light as is needed to see well. A domestic cat's pupils close down to slits, while most big cats' pupils close to tiny circles.

◄ GLOWING EYES
Like other cats, the leopard has a reflective layer called the tapetum at the back of e
eye. This reflects light back into the e
giving the nerve cells extra stimulat
so that they send stronger signals
the brain. The reflection causes
eyes to glow when light shin
into them at night.

PREY IN SIGHT ▶

As it stalks through the long grass a lion must pounce at just the right moment if it is to catch its prey. Because a cat's eyes are set slightly apart at the front of the head, their field of view overlaps. This means the cat has binocular vision, which enables it to judge the exact position of its prey so it knows when to strike.

▲ ROUND-EYED

This puma's rounded pupils have closed down in daylight. In dim light, the pupils will expand wide to let in as much light as possible.

Large earflaps concentrate sound waves deep into each ear.

SHARP EARS ▶

Cats' ears are designed for them to hear very well. This Siberian lynx lives in snowy forests where the sound is often muffled. It has specially-shaped, big ears to catch as much sound as possible.

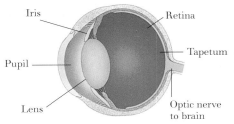

Iris — Retina

Pupil — — Tapetum

Lens — Optic nerve to brain

▲ INSIDE THE EYE

The lens focuses light rays to produce a sharp image on the retina. Impulses from the retina are carried to the brain by the optic nerve. Cats have a membrane that can be pulled over the surface of the eye to keep out dirt and dust.

Touching, Tasting and Smelling

Like all animals, cats can feel things by touching them with their skin, but they have another important touching tool – whiskers. These long, stiff hairs on the face have very sensitive nerve endings at their roots. Some whiskers are for protection. Anything brushing against the whiskers above a cat's eyes will make it blink. A cat's tongue is a useful tool and its nose is very sensitive. Cats use smell and taste to communicate with each other. Thin, curled bones in the nose carry scents inwards to smell receptors. Cats also have a chemical detector called a Jacobson's organ in the roof of the mouth to distinguish scents, especially those of other cats.

▲ **TONGUE TOOL**
A leopard curls the tip of its tongue like a spoon to lap up water. After several laps it will drink the water in one gulp. As well as drinking, the tongue is used for tasting, scraping meat off a carcass and grooming.

◀ **ROUGH TONGUE**
A tiger's bright pink tongue has a very rough surface. Cats' tongues are covered with small spikes called papillae. The papillae point backwards and are used by the cat, together with its teeth, to strip meat off bones. Around the edge and at the back of the tongue are taste buds. Cats cannot taste sweet things, but they can recognize pure water.

The tiger raises its head and grimaces to taste the air.

Cats twitch their tails from side to side as they concentrate. When angry, the tail lashes to and fro.

WHO PASSED BY? ▶

By tasting the air a tiger uses its Jacobson's organ (the special scent centre in the roof of the mouth) to detect the scent left by another tiger. To get as much of the scent as it can, it wrinkles its nose, curls its lips upwards, bares its teeth and lifts its head. This action is known as flehmen. Males use it especially to locate females ready to mate.

Did you know? Hairballs coughed up by lions are worn as talismans in some parts of Africa.

▲ THE CAT'S WHISKERS

This snow leopard's face is surrounded by sensitive whiskers. Cats use their whiskers to sense nearby objects and air movements. The most important whiskers are on the sides of the face. These help a cat to feel its way in the dark, or when it is walking through tall grass.

▼ COAT CARE

The long, rough tongue of a lion makes a very good comb. It removes loose hairs and combs the fur flat and straight. Cats wipe their faces, coats and paws clean. They spend a lot of time looking after their fur. Hair swallowed during grooming is spat out as hairballs.

107

On the Prowl

Cats run and jump easily and gracefully. They have flexible spines and strong hind legs. With long, bouncy strides, they can cover the ground very quickly. Big cats are not good long-distance runners, but are great sprinters and pouncers. They use their long tails for balance when climbing trees and running fast. All cats can swim very well, but some prefer to avoid getting wet and will only swim to escape danger. Others, such as tigers and jaguars, live near water and often swim to hunt their prey.

▲ THRILL OF THE CHASE

A lion chases its prey through the scrub. When lions stalk, run and pounce, they make use of their flexible backs, strong back legs, powerful chests and cushioning pads under their paws. Cats' back legs are especially powerful. They provide the major thrust for running. Cats can outpace their prey over short distances before launching into a final jump.

◀ TREE-CLIMBING CAT

Leopards spend a lot of time in trees and are designed for climbing. They have very powerful chests and front legs. Their shoulder blades are positioned to the side to make them better climbers. A leopard can leap 3m without difficulty and, in exceptional circumstances, can leap over 6m.

◄ **SOFT PADDING**

The thick pads under a lion's paw are like cushions. They allow the lion to move very quietly and also act as shock absorbers when running and jumping. Hidden between the pads and fur are the lion's claws, tucked away safely until they are needed.

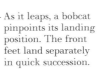

Did you know? In the 1500s, rich people kept cheetahs as hunting animals like dogs.

GRACE AND AGILITY ►

A bobcat leaps with great agility off a rock. All cats have flexible backs and short collarbones to help make their bodies stronger for jumping and landing. Bobcats are similar to lynxes. Both cats have an extensive coating of fur on their feet to give them extra warmth. The fur also prevents them from slipping on icy rocks.

As it leaps, a bobcat pinpoints its landing position. The front feet land separately in quick succession.

◄ **KEEPING COOL**

A Bengal tiger swims gracefully across a river. Most tigers live in warm areas, such as India and South-east Asia. As well as swimming to get from one place to another, they often look for pools of water to bathe in during the heat of the day. They are one of the few cats that actively enjoy being in or near water. Tigers are excellent swimmers and can easily cross a lake 5km wide.

Eyes of the Wolf

Dogs have excellent hearing. They can hear the sound of a snapping twig over 3km away and are alert to the smallest noise that might give away the presence of potential prey. They also hear a wider range of sounds than humans. They can hear ultrasounds (very high-pitched sounds) that are too high for human ears to detect. This means they can track down mice and other rodents in the dark. Sight is less important than hearing for hunting. Wolves are good at spotting movement, even at a great distance, but find it harder to see objects that keep still. Wild dogs that hunt at night rely on sound and smell rather than sight. African hunting dogs and dholes (relations of the wolf), however, hunt by day, often in open country, and have keener sight.

Coyote
(*Canis latrans*)

▲ PRICKED EARS
Wolves cock (turn) their ears in different directions to pinpoint distant sounds. Even a tiny noise betrays the hiding place of a victim.

▲ LISTENING IN
An African hunting dog's large, rounded ears work like satellite dishes to gather sound. Keen hearing is vital in the hunt and allows pack members to keep in touch among the tall grass.

HOWLING HELLO ▶
Coyotes and other wild dogs keep in touch with distant members of their group by howling. The coyote call is actually a series of yelps that ends in a long wail.

110

◄ BARKING MAD
Some domestic dogs, such as this German shepherd, have been bred to bark loudly to warn their owners of approaching strangers. Wolves also bark if they meet an intruder near the den, but more quietly and less aggressively.

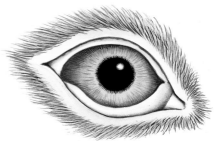

▲ A THIRD EYELID
Wolves' eyes have a third eyelid, called a nictitating (blinking) membrane. This membrane is inside their upper and lower eyelids, and sweeps over the surface of the eye when the wolf blinks. It protects the eyes from dust and dirt that might damage it otherwise.

◄ GLOWING EYES
Wolves have round, yellow eyes. As with cats, in dark conditions, a reflective layer at the back of the eye, the tapetum, intensifies what little light there is. This allows a wolf to see at night. If a strong light is shone into a wolf's eyes, the reflection gives the eyes an eerie glow.

100°   *270°*

human   wolf

◄ WOLF VISION
Wide-set eyes in the front of its face give a wolf a very wide field of vision. As the view from each eye overlaps, binocular vision (using both eyes at the same time) allows a wolf to judge distances and locate its prey.

A Keen Sense of Smell

Of all the senses, smell is the most important for wolves and other wild dogs. These animals are constantly surrounded by different scents and their keen sense of smell can distinguish them all. They follow the scent trails left behind by other animals in their quest for food, and can pick up even faint whiffs of scent on the wind. This helps them to figure out the direction of distant prey. Wild dogs that hunt in packs use scent to identify and communicate with other pack members. They also communicate by sight and touch. Like other mammals, wolves and wild dogs have taste buds on their tongues to taste their food. They eat foods they find the tastiest first. The tongue is also used to lap up water.

▲ **TRACKING PREY**
Nose to the ground, a wolf follows a scent trail on the ground. From the scent a wolf can tell what type of animal left it, whether it is well or ill, how long ago it passed by and whether another wolf is following the trail.

▶ **ON THE SCENT**
Bloodhounds were specially bred as tracking dogs. They have a very acute sense of smell and can follow a scent that is several days old. They keep their noses very close to the ground. Their drooping ears help to channel scent into the nose.

▲ **PLEASED TO MEET YOU**
When two wolves meet they sniff the glands at the base of the tail. Pack members all have a familiar scent. Scent is also used to signal mood, such as contentment or fear, or if a female is ready to breed.

112

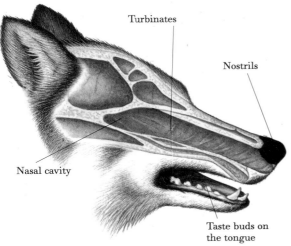

Turbinates

Nostrils

Nasal cavity

Taste buds on
the tongue

▲ TOUCHY-FEELY

Wolves use touch to bond with each other.
They rub bodies, lick one another and thrust
their noses into each other's fur when they
meet. Pack members play-fight by wrestling
with locked jaws, or chasing around in circles.

▲ INSIDE THE SNOUT

Inside a wolf's snout is a large nasal cavity used
for smelling. Scent particles pass over tubes of
very thin bone in the roof of the nasal cavity.
These tubes, called turbinates, are connected to
a nerve network that sends signals to the brain.

▼ SENSITIVE NOSE

The wolf's leathery outer nose is set
right at the end of
its snout. Two
nostrils draw air
laden with scents into
the nasal cavity. The
wolf may flare its
nostrils to take in extra
air. The animal may
lick its nose before
scenting, because a
damp nose helps its
sense of smell. Long,
sensitive whiskers on
either side of the
snout are used for
touching things
at close range.

▲ WELL GROOMED

A wolf nibbles at the tufts of hair
between its paw pads. It is
removing ice that might cut and
damage the paw. Wolves groom
(clean) their fur to keep it in good
condition. Licking and running
fur through the teeth helps to
remove dirt and dislodge fleas.

113

Running Wild

Wild dogs are tireless runners. Wolves can lope along for hours on end at a steady pace of 40km/h without resting. They have been known to cover an amazing 200km in a day searching for food. Compared to cheetahs, which can reach speeds of about 100km/h over short distances, wolves are not fast runners. They can, however, put on a burst of speed to overtake fleeing prey.

Wolves and most other dogs have four toes on their back feet and five toes on their front feet. The fifth toe on the front foot is called the dew claw, a small, functionless claw located a little way up on the back of each front leg. It is more like a pad than a claw. Dogs also have tough pads on the underside of their toes to help absorb the impact as their feet hit the ground.

▲ SPEEDING COYOTE
Like wolves, coyotes are good long-distance runners. They run on their toes, like other dogs. This helps them to take long strides and so cover more ground. If necessary, coyotes can trot along for hours in search of food.

Did you know? Studies of wolves in the U.S. show one pack travelled 1100km in 40 days.

◄ IN MID-LEAP
Strong leg muscles enable a wolf to leap long distances – up to 4.5m in a single bound. Wolves and other dogs are very agile and can leap upwards, sideways and even backwards. As the wolf lands, its toes splay out to support its weight and prevent it from slipping.

Grey wolf
(Canis lupus)

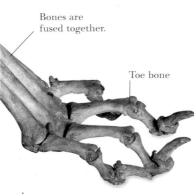

LONG TOE ▶

This close-up of the bones in a maned wolf's foreleg shows the long foot bones and the long toe bones that are used for walking. The foot bones between the ankle joint and the toes are fused together for greater strength.

Ankle joint

Bones are fused together.

Toe bone

▲ WOLF TRACK

Clawmarks show up clearly in a line of wolf prints in a snowy landscape. Unlike cats, wolves and other wild dogs cannot retract (draw in) their claws. When walking, the wolf places its paws almost in a straight line, to form a single track. The pawprints of a running wolf are more widely spaced.

IN THE WATER ▶

Bush dogs make their homes near streams and rivers and spend much of their lives in water. They are strong swimmers, and water creatures such as capybaras (a large type of rodent) form part of their diet. Wolves, dingoes and most other dogs can also swim well.

A KEEN CLIMBER ▶

Wolves and wild dogs are quick on the ground, but they cannot climb trees. Some foxes, however, climb well. The grey fox of North America is an expert climber. It scrambles up trees to steal birds' eggs and chicks. It also climbs to get a good view over surrounding countryside when searching for prey.

Grey fox

(*Urocyon cinereoargenteus*)

115

The World of Apes

Apes are creatures of the daytime and their most important sense is their keen eyesight. Their forward-facing eyes can pick up fine detail, judge distances and see in colour. Their nose is a small, but useful, back-up to the eyes. Their sense of smell is probably better than that of humans. Apes sniff food and each other and also use their sense of smell to warn them of something unusual in their environment. If they do not recognize a smell, or if it makes them uneasy, they will use their eyes to investigate. The fact that apes rely more on sight than smell may be one reason why they have little hair on their faces. Facial expressions are easier to see without hair getting in the way, so they can be used as visual signals for communication.

▲ **EXCELLENT EYES**

The eyes of apes, such as this young orangutan, are set close together, facing forwards. This enables both eyes to focus on the same object. The signals from each eye are combined by the ape's brain to produce three-dimensional images for judging distance and depth accurately.

◄ **NOSEPRINTS** ►

Individual gorillas can be identified by the shape of their noses. The folds, wrinkles and outline of a gorilla's nose are just as distinctive as its fingerprint. Each of the three kinds of gorilla also has a different nose shape. These differences are especially clear when the nose of the mountain gorilla (*left*) is compared with that of a western lowland gorilla (*right*).

▲ SENSITIVE SKIN

Like humans, gorillas have tiny raised ridges, or fingerprints, on the tips of their fingers. These ridges help gorillas feel and grip on to objects. Each gorilla's fingerprint is unique. Flat nails protect the sensitive fingertips from damage. A gorilla's hands respond to temperature and pressure as well as to touch.

Did you know? Male orangutans use a long call to keep other males away and to attract females.

Three Wise Monkeys

A set of three Japanese monkeys were once used to explain Buddhist teachings. One monkey is covering its ears – this one represents the idea of 'hear no evil'. Another has its hands over its eyes so that it can see no evil. The third is stopping words from coming out of its mouth – representing the third wise saying of 'speak no evil'.

NOISY APE ▶

Gibbons rely greatly on sound for communicating among the leafy treetops. When the siamang sings, its throat pouch swells up with air. This pouch of air acts like a resonating chamber to make its call even louder. Some other gibbons have these pouches, too, but not such big ones.

▼ SOUND SENSE

Big ears help chimpanzees to pick up the sounds drifting through the forest. They often stop and listen for the sounds of chimps or other animals, which may tell them of approaching danger. They also hoot to each other to keep in contact.

Apes on the Move

To an ape, the tangle of trunks, branches and vines in a forest is like a gigantic climbing frame that provides high-level walkways through the air. Gibbons, orangutans and bonobos spend a lot of time in the trees. Large male orangutans also travel on the ground some of the time because of their great weight. The true masters of treetop travel are the gibbons, able to leap and swing effortlessly across gaps at great speed and at great heights. Chimpanzees and gorillas are mainly ground-based creatures, although chimpanzees often climb trees to find food and may spend the night in the branches. Gorillas, even with their great bulk, sometimes venture into trees.

▲ KNUCKLE WALKING

On the ground, chimpanzees and gorillas rest their weight on pads of thick skin on their knuckles. This is called knuckle walking.

▲ CLIMBING CHIMP

Chimpanzees climb into the trees to find leaves or fruit to eat, to chase prey and to build sleeping nests. Their long fingers hook over the branches and give them a good grip for both climbing and swinging.

Tarzan of the Apes
American writer Edgar Rice Burroughs created the character Tarzan in a magazine story published in 1912. Tarzan is orphaned as a baby in the jungles of Africa. A tribe of apes takes care of him, teaching him how to survive in the jungle and swing through trees. He shares his later adventures with his wife Jane and their son Korak.

118

**Orangutans
(*Pongo pygmaeus*)**

◄ **FLEXIBLE APE**

When climbing, the body weight of an orangutan is evenly spread between its arms and legs. This helps the orangutan to keep its balance. The shoulder and hip joints of an orangutan are very supple, allowing it to stretch easily between branches. Orangutans can even eat hanging upside-down. They will sway slender trees until they can reach far enough to catch a branch on the next tree. They often make a lot of noise.

Did you know? A gorilla can run at 25-33km/h over short distances.

◄ **SWINGING GIBBONS**

With their extraordinarily long arms, gibbons swing at breathtaking speed from branch to branch, often leaping huge distances. Special wrist bones allow a gibbon to turn its body as it swings without loosening its grip. This means it can swing hand-over-hand in a speedy swing, known as brachiating. Compared with the noisy crashings of monkeys leaping from tree to tree, gibbons are almost silent travellers.

▲ **GRIPPING FEAT**

Gorillas are wary tree climbers and rarely swing by their arms like orangutans or gibbons. They climb down from a tree backwards, holding the trunk loosely with both feet in a controlled slide.

119

The Senses of Small Primates

Monkeys and apes are usually active in the daytime, and make the most of their excellent colour vision. Most other primates, known as prosimians, move around at night, and have eyes that can see in the dark. All primate eyes contain cone cells and rod cells, but monkeys have more colour-sensitive cone cells in their eyes. The eyes of prosimians have plenty of rod cells, that work in dim light. Their eyes glow in the dark because most prosimians' eyes are backed by a mirror-like layer that reflects the light.

Sight is very important to monkeys and apes, but other primates rely much more on smelling and hearing. The ears of prosimians are constantly on the alert. The slightest rustle in the dark could identify an insect snack or an approaching predator.

▲ COLOUR SELECTION
Thanks to its colour vision, a vervet monkey can select the tastiest flowers when they are at the peak of perfection. Many leaf-eating monkeys have eyes that are particularly sensitive to different shades of green. This means that they can easily identify the fresh green of tender young leaves which are good to eat.

MIDNIGHT MONKEY ▶
Douroucouli monkeys are the only nocturnal (night-active) monkeys. They live in South America where there are no other nocturnal primates to compete with. Their eyes are big to catch maximum light. They are able to pick up detail but not colour.

▲ EYES LIKE SAUCERS
Unlike the eyes of many prosimians, tarsiers' eyes have no reflective layer, but their size means they catch as much light as possible. Like monkeys, their eyes have a sensitive area called the fovea, which picks out very sharp detail.

▼ A KEEN SENSE OF SMELL

An emperor tamarin monkey marks its territory with scent. American monkeys and most prosimians have a smelling organ in the roof of their mouths that monkeys from elsewhere do not have. They use their sense of smell to communicate with each other and to identify food that is good and ready to eat.

▲ WET-NOSED SMELLING AIDS

Look at the shiny nose of this ruffed lemur. It is more like that of a dog than a monkey. Most prosimians have this moist nostril and lip area, called the rhinarium. It gives them a better sense of smell. The nose has a layer of cells that detect chemicals in the air. The cells work better when they are wet.

▼ MUFFLED SENSE OF HEARING

The furry ears of squirrel monkeys probably muffle sound. But although these and other monkeys use sound to communicate with each other, hearing is not as important for them as keen eyesight. Nocturnal primates, however, have highly sensitive, delicate-skinned ears.

Brain Waves in the Sea

A whale controls its body through its nervous system. The brain is the control centre, carrying out many functions automatically, but also acting upon information supplied by the senses. The sizes of whale brains vary according to the animals' sizes. However, dolphins have much bigger brains for their size. Hearing is by far a whale's most important sense, it picks up sounds with tiny ears located just behind the eyes.

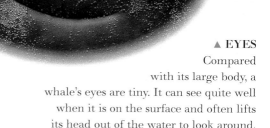

▲ EYES
Compared with its large body, a whale's eyes are tiny. It can see quite well when it is on the surface and often lifts its head out of the water to look around.

Did you know? A sperm whale's brain is five times the size of a human's.

◀ CLOSE ENCOUNTERS
A group of Atlantic spotted dolphins swim closely together in the seas around the Bahamas (Atlantic islands). Like most other whales, the dolphins nudge one another and stroke each other with their flippers and tail. Touch plays a very important part in dolphin society, especially in courtship.

◄ SLAP HAPPY

A humpback whale slapping its tail, or lob-tailing, a favourite pastime for large whales. Lob-tailing creates a noise like a gunshot in the air, but, more importantly, it will make a loud crash underwater. All the other whales in the area will be able to hear the noise.

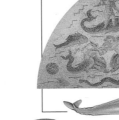

Cupids and Dolphins
In this Roman mosaic, cupids and dolphins gambol together. In Roman mythology, Cupid was the god of love. Roman artists were inspired by the dolphin's intelligence and gentleness. They regarded them as sacred creatures.

◄ BRAINY DOLPHIN?

Some dolphins, such as the bottlenose, have a complex brain with many folds, much the same size as our own. However, scientists are still not sure how intelligent dolphins really are.

► IN TRAINING

A bottlenose dolphin is shown with its trainer. This species has a particularly large brain for its size. It can be easily trained and has a good memory. It can observe other animals and learn to mimic their behaviour in a short space of time. It is also good at solving problems, something we consider a sign of intelligence.

Swim and Splash

All whales are superb swimmers. All parts of the whale's body help it move through the water. The driving force comes from tail fins, or flukes. Using very powerful muscles in the rear third of its body, the whale beats its tail up and down and the whole body bends. It uses its pectoral fins, or flippers, near the front of the body to steer with. The body itself is almost hairless to make it streamlined and smooth so it can slip through the water easily. The body can change shape slightly to keep the water flowing smoothly around it.

▲ STEERING
Among whales, the humpback has by far the longest front flippers. As well as for steering, it uses its flippers for slapping the water. Flipper-slapping seems to be a form of communication.

◄ TAIL POWER
The tail flukes of a grey whale rise into the air before it dives. Whales move their broad tails up and down to drive themselves through the water.

▼ MASSIVE FIN
The dorsal fin of a killer whale (orca) projects high into the air. The animal is a swift swimmer, and the fin helps keep its body well balanced. The killer whale has such a large dorsal fin that some experts believe it may help to regulate its body temperature, or even be used in courtship. Many whales and dolphins have a dorsal fin, and others only have a raised hump.

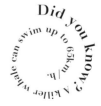

Did you know? A killer whale can swim up to 65km/h.

◄ STREAMLINING
Atlantic spotted dolphins' bodies are beautifully streamlined – shaped so that they slip easily through the water when they move. The dolphin's body is long and rounded, broad in front and becoming narrower towards the tail. Apart from the dorsal fin and flippers, nothing projects from its body. It has no external ears or rear limbs.

▼ HOW A DOLPHIN SWIMS
Dolphins beat their tail flukes up and down by means of the powerful muscles near the tail. The flukes force the water backwards at each stroke. As the water is forced back, the dolphin's body is forced forwards. Its other fins help guide it through the water. They do not provide propulsion.

◄ SMOOTH-SKINNED
This bottlenose dolphin is tailwalking – supporting itself by powerful thrusts of its tail. Unlike most mammals, it has very few hairs or hair follicles – the dimples in the skin from which the hair grows. Its smooth skin helps the dolphin's body slip through the water.

▼ HOW A FISH SWIMS
It is mainly the tail that provides the power for a fish to swim. The tail has vertical fins, unlike a dolphin's horizontal flukes. It swims by beating its tail and body from side to side.

The Senses of a Killer

A shark's brain is small for its size, but its senses are highly developed. Sharks see well, and see in colour. They can also recognize shapes. Just as amazing are a different range of senses that allow sharks to pick up sounds and vibrations from great distances. They can detect changes in the ocean currents, recognize smells and follow the trail of a smell right back to its source. Some species have shiny plates at the backs of their eyes that collect light to help them see as they dive to deep, dark water. They also have dark-coloured membranes that they draw across the shiny plates to avoid being dazzled by the light when they return to the surface. Sharks even have special nerves in their noses that can detect minute electrical fields, such as those produced by the muscles of their fish prey.

▲ ELECTRICAL SENSE
Like all sharks, sandtiger sharks have tiny pits in their snouts, known as the ampullae of Lorenzini. Inside these pits are special nerves. These help the shark to find food by detecting minute electrical fields in the muscles of its prey.

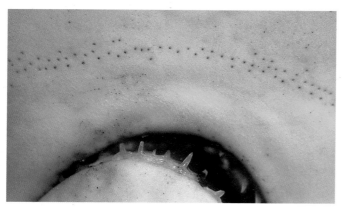

◄ PREY DETECTOR
In a hammerhead shark the special pits that can sense electrical fields in its prey are spread across the hammer of the shark's head, helping it to scan for prey across a wide area. The hammerhead searches for food by sweeping its head from side to side, rather as if using a metal detector. It can find any prey buried in the sand below.

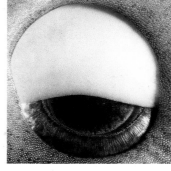

◀ SIGHT, SMELL AND SOUND

The nostrils of the hammerhead shark are positioned wide apart on its head. This gives the shark 'stereo smelling' with which it can more easily track odours to their source. But, because its eyes are at the ends of its hammer, it must turn its head from side to side in order to see forwards.

Scalloped hammerhead shark (*Sphyrna lewini*)

▲ EYE PROTECTION

When a shark bites, its eyes can easily be injured by the victim's teeth, spines or claws. To prevent this, sharks such as this tiger shark have a special membrane (sheath) that slides down across the eye during the attack.

Eye of blacktip reef shark

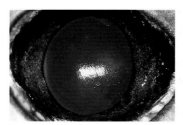

Eye of bluntnose sixgill shark

◀ DEEP AND SHALLOW

The blacktip reef shark has a small eye with a narrow, vertical slit. This type of eye is often found in shallow-water sharks. Sharks that swim in deeper waters, such as the sixgill shark, tend to have large, round pupils.

Did you know? Sharks find their way through mazes as fast as rabbits.

Shark Callers

On the islands of the south-west Pacific, sharks are the islanders' gods. To test their manhood, young shark callers attract sharks by shaking a coconut rattle under the water. Sensing the vibrations, a shark will swim close to the canoe. It is then wrestled into the boat, and its meat divided among the villagers as a gift from the gods.

Amazing Animals

Every animal is stalked, chased or attacked at some point in its life by another animal. This section shows how a balance between instinct and learning helps it to survive those incidents, and reveals that some animals go to extraordinary extremes to outwit their aggressors.

Amazing Animals

Insects with built-in flash-lights, spiders producing silk as strong as steel wire, and elephants with noses powerful enough to lift tree trunks and yet sensitive enough to pick up small coins — these are just a few of nature's truly amazing animals. You can add snakes that swallow animals bigger than themselves, bears with compasses in their heads, and birds that find their way from Europe to Africa and back every year.

Thick fur over the body, including the face, insulates bears and allows them to live in some of the world's coldest places.

Evolution and Adaptation

Like all animal characteristics, these amazing features have developed by evolution. This is a gradual change in physical appearance, body chemistry or behaviour from generation to generation. Babies inherit many of their parents' features, so any change that makes an animal more successful at feeding or evading its enemies is likely to be passed on. A change that makes an animal less successful is unlikely to be passed on, because the animal will either die or will not have so many babies. Only the fittest animals survive. The changes between one generation and the next may be very small, but they can add up to big changes over time, so the animals get more specialized at what they do.

As a result of millions of years of evolution, plants and animals have adapted to live almost everywhere on earth. We are surrounded by a variety of animals and plants, and each kind is perfectly suited to the challenges in its life. Everything about an owl, for example, is geared to its role as a nocturnal predator (night active hunter). Its big eyes take in the greatest possible amount of light, its keen ears can pick up the slightest sound and its soft feathers let the bird fly silently without alerting prey.

The crocodile's body and habits are so successful that it hasn't changed in millions of years.

Acting by Instinct

Weird shapes and intricate colour patterns help to
hide or protect many animals from their enemies, but
it is their behaviour that makes so many animals really
amazing – especially when you realize that most
of them do things automatically. Fireflies, for
example, do not have to learn how to flash
their lights in the correct sequence, and
spiders never have web-building lessons,
yet they perform this perfectly every
time. In-built behaviour patterns of this
kind are called instincts and they are
inherited in just the same way as the animals' shapes and colours.

*Cats are born with a hunting
instinct. They keep watch and
crouch near to the ground,
waiting to pounce on their prey.*

   Instinctive activities are usually triggered by some kind of signal
or stimulus from the surroundings or from another animal. For
example, a rattlesnake rattles when it detects the vibrations caused
by a large animal, and the caterpillar of a swallowtail butterfly
releases a very strong smell when it is touched by a predator or a parasite (an animal living on
or in another). The migration of the majority of birds is triggered by the increase or decrease in
the number of daylight hours. Many mammals prepare for hibernation (an inactive state during
the winter) when the days grow shorter in the autumn, while the mass migration of mammals,
including the huge grazing herds of the African plains, is usually set off when suitable food
becomes scarce. Simple hunger, however, can also stimulate animals to hunt for food.

The Ability to Learn

The lives of most animals are ruled entirely by instinct, with a given stimulus always producing
the same reaction. However, many birds and mammals, with their complex brains, can change

their behaviour by learning. Although cats and other predatory
mammals may chase prey instinctively, it is only by watching
their parents that they can learn to hunt properly. Monkeys and
apes have some of the best learning skills. Chimps can solve
simple problems, such as how to stack a pile of blocks to
reach something that is high up. Using their creative brains
and nimble fingers, they can even invent and use tools.

Stuck in the Past

Evolution continues and many animals are constantly adapting
to changing conditions, but some species have hardly changed
for millions of years. Crocodiles evolved their protective armour
long ago and probably because they can go for so long without
food, they survived the disaster that wiped out the dinosaurs
65 million years ago. Crocodiles are often known as living fossils.

*When a monkey or ape discovers a
new skill, others learn by watching
and then trying it out themselves.*

Insect Defences

The naturalist Charles Darwin's theory of evolution explains how only the best-adapted animals survive to breed and pass on their characteristics to the next generation. The key to survival is escaping danger. Beetles and bugs have many enemies in the natural world. They also have many ways of avoiding attack. Many species run, fly, hop or swim away, but some species are also armed with weapons. Some bugs and beetles can bite or use sharp spines for protection. Others are armed with poisonous fluids or taste nasty. These insects are often brightly coloured, which tells predators such as birds to stay away.

▲ **PRICKLY CUSTOMER**
This weevil from the island of Madagascar has an impressive array of sharp spines on its back. Few predators will try such a prickly morsel – if they do, the pain may make them drop their meal!

▼ **LITTLE STINKER**
Squash bugs are also known as stink bugs because of the smelly liquid they produce to ward off enemies. Like other insects, squash bugs do not actively *decide* to defend themselves. Instead, they instinctively react when their sense organs tell them that danger is near.

▲ **READY TO SHOOT**
Desert skunk beetles defend themselves by shooting a foul-smelling spray from their abdomens. This beetle has taken up a defensive posture by balancing on its head with its abdomen raised in the air. It is ready to fire its spray if an intruder comes close. Most predators will back away.

▼ TRICKY BEETLE

The devil's coach-horse beetle has several ways of defending itself from attack. First, it raises its tail in a pose that mimics a stinging scorpion (below). This defence is a trick, for the beetle cannot sting. If the trick does not work, the beetle gives off an unpleasant smell to send its enemies reeling. If all else fails, it delivers a painful bite with its large jaws.

devil's coach-horse beetle
(Staphylinus olens)

Blistering Attack

The blister beetle gives off a chemical that causes human and animal skin to blister. Centuries ago, the chemical was thought to cure warts. Doctors applied blister beetles to the skin of patients suffering from the infection. The 'cure' was probably painful and did not work.

◄ PLAYING DEAD

This beetle from East Africa is trying to fool an enemy by playing dead. It drops to the ground and lies on its back with its legs curled in a lifeless position. This defence works well on enemies that eat only live prey. However, it does not work on the many predators that are not fussy whether their victims are alive or dead.

WARNING COLOURS ►

The cardinal beetle's body contains chemicals that have a terrible taste to predators. The beetle's blood-red colour helps to warn its enemies away. This colour coding will only work if the predator has tried to eat another beetle of the same species. If so, it will recognize the species by its colour and leave it alone.

cardinal beetle
(Pyrochroa coccinea)

Focus on

At nightfall in warm countries, the darkness may be lit up by hundreds of tiny, flashing yellow-green lights. The lights are produced by insects called fireflies. There are over 1,000 different types of firefly, but not all species glow in the dark. The light is produced by special organs in the insects' abdomens. Fireflies are nocturnal (night-active) beetles. Some species, known as glow-worms, produce a continuous greenish glow, while others flash their lights on and off. These signals are all designed for one purpose – to attract a mate in the darkness.

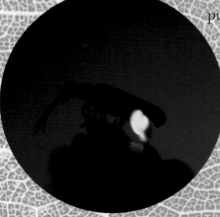

FIREFLY BY DAY

Fireflies are flat and slender. Most are dark brown or black, with orange or yellow markings. The light organs are found in their abdomens. Most firefly species have two pairs of wings.

PRODUCING LIGHT

A male firefly flashes his light to females nearby. He produces light when chemicals mix in his abdomen, causing a reaction that releases energy in the form of light. In deep oceans many sea creatures, such as fish and squid, produce light in a similar way.

CODED SIGNALS

A female firefly climbs on to a grass stem to signal with her glowing tail. Each species of firefly has its own sequence of flashes, which serves as a private mating code. On warm summer evenings, the wingless females send this code to the flashing males that fly above.

Fireflies

FALSE CODE FOR HUNTING

Most adult fireflies feed on flower nectar or do not eat at all. However, the female of this North American species is a meat-eater – and her prey is other fireflies. When the flightless female sees a male firefly of a different species circling overhead, she flashes his response code to attract him to the ground. When he lands nearby, she pounces and eats him. She also flashes to males of her own species to attract them to her for mating.

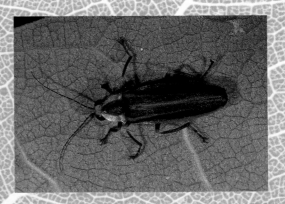

LIT UP LIKE A CHRISTMAS TREE

A group of fireflies light up a tree by a bridge as they signal to one another. In parts of Asia, some species of fireflies gather in large groups on trees. When one insect, called the pacemaker, flashes its light, all of the other fireflies on the tree begin to flash their lights at the same time and to the same pattern. When this happens, the whole tree can be seen to glow and pulse with brilliant flashes of light.

YOUNG FIREFLY

Like the adults, firefly larvae also make light although their lamps are not usually very bright. Young fireflies hatch from eggs laid in moist places by the females. Unlike most of their parents, all firefly larvae are meat-eaters. They kill slugs and snails by injecting them with powerful digestive juices. These dissolve the flesh and the firefly larvae suck up the resulting solution through their hollow jaws. The young fireflies never have wings.

135

Six Lively Legs

Not all insects can fly, but they can all move around and even climb trees using their six legs. Social insects, such as wasps and bees, use their legs to groom (clean) their bodies as well.

All insects belong to a larger group of animals called arthropods, which means 'jointed legs'. True to this name, adult insects have legs with many joints in them. An insect's legs have four main sections – the coxa, femur, tibia and tarsus. The coxa is the top part of the leg, joined to the thorax. The femur corresponds to the thigh, and the tibia is the lower leg. The tarsus, or foot, is made up of several smaller sections. Insects' legs do not have bones. Instead, they are supported by hard outer cases, like hollow tubes.

Did you know? Adult insects have six legs, but young bees, wasps and ants have no legs at all.

▲ **GRIPPING STUFF**
This magnified photograph of a bee's foot shows clearly the tiny claws on the end of its foot. Claws help insects to grip smooth surfaces such as shiny leaves, stems and branches, and stop them from slipping. Ants can walk along the underside of leaves with the help of their claws.

STILT WALKER ▶
Like other ants, this Australian bulldog ant has legs made up of several long, thin sections. In the hot, dry areas of Australia, the ant's stilt-like legs raise her high above the hot, dusty ground, helping to keep her cool. As well as walking, climbing and running, insects' legs have other uses. Some ants and termites use their legs to dig underground burrows. Bees carry food home on their hind legs.

▲ MULTI-PURPOSE LEGS

Bees use their legs to grip on to flowers and also to walk, carry nesting materials and clean their furry bodies. Their front legs have special notches to clean their antennae. They use their hind legs to carry pollen back to the nest.

▲ ON THE MOVE

Army ants spend their whole lives on the move. Instead of building permanent nests as other ants do, they march through the forest in search of prey, attacking any creature they find and scavenging from dead carcasses.

▼ EXPERT CLIMBERS

Termites swarm along a tree branch in Malaysia, South-east Asia. Many termites nest underground, but some build their nests high in trees. They climb vertical tree trunks by digging their claws into the bark.

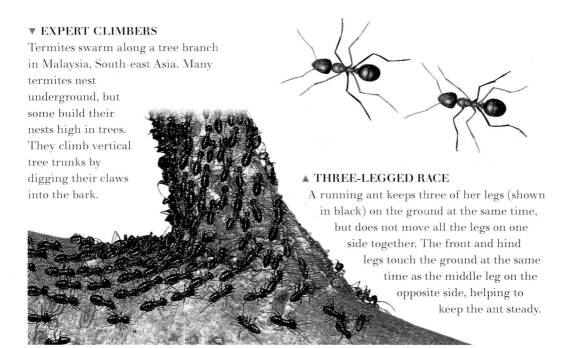

▲ THREE-LEGGED RACE

A running ant keeps three of her legs (shown in black) on the ground at the same time, but does not move all the legs on one side together. The front and hind legs touch the ground at the same time as the middle leg on the opposite side, helping to keep the ant steady.

Chemical Warfare

African euchromia moth
(Euchromia lethe)

Most butterflies and moths escape their enemies by avoiding being spotted. However, some use other tricks. They cannot sting or bite like bees or wasps, but many caterpillars have different ways of using toxic chemicals to poison their attackers, or at least make themselves unpleasant to taste or smell. For example, the caterpillar of the brown-tail moth has barbed hairs tipped with a poison that can cause a severe skin rash even in humans. A cinnabar moth cannot poison a predator, but it tastes foul if eaten. Usually, caterpillars that are unpalatable to predators are brightly coloured to let potential attackers know that they should be avoided.

▲ BRIGHT AND DEADLY

The brilliant colours of the African euchromia moth warn any would-be predators that it is poisonous. It also has an awful smell. Some moths manufacture their own poisons, but others are toxic because their caterpillars eat poisonous plants. The poisons do not hurt the insects, but make them harmful to their enemies.

▲ HAIRY MOUTHFUL

The caterpillar of the sycamore moth is bright yellow. It is not poisonous like some of the other brightly coloured caterpillars, but its masses of long, hairy tufts make it distinctly unpleasant to eat.

▼ THREATENING DISPLAY

The caterpillar of the puss moth may look clown-like and harmless, but by caterpillar standards it is quite fearsome. When threatened, its slender whip-like tails are thrust forwards and it may squirt a jet of harmful formic acid from a gland near its mouth. It also uses red markings and false eye spots on its head to create an aggressive display.

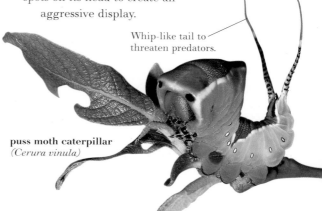

Whip-like tail to threaten predators.

puss moth caterpillar
(Cerura vinula)

◄ POISONOUS MILK

A Monarch butterfly caterpillar feeds on various kinds of milkweed, which contain a powerful poison. This chemical is harmful to many small creatures. The poison stays in the Monarch's body throughout its life. This may be why Monarchs show less fear of predators than other butterflies.

► RED ALERT

The striking red, white and black colours of the spurge hawk moth caterpillar tell that it is poisonous. Unpalatable insects often display conspicuous colours such as reds, yellows, black and white. These insects do not need to protect themselves by blending into their background. This caterpillar acquires its poison from a plant called spurge, which it feeds on.

spurge hawk moth caterpillar
(Hyles euphorbiae)

Did you know? Many harmless butterflies mimic poisonous species so well that enemies dare not touch them.

▼ SMELLY CATERPILLAR

The swallowtail caterpillar produces an odour that is strong enough to ward off parasites. It comes from a scent-gland called the osmeterium situated just behind its head. This gland suddenly erupts and oozes acid when the caterpillar is threatened.

swallowtail caterpillar
(Papilio machaon)

▲ DEFENSIVE FROTH

Rhodogastria moths of Australasia and Africa often have a bright red abdomen to warn enemies that they carry a deadly poison. When the moth is threatened, this poison oozes out from a gland on the back of its neck.

139

Fabulous

Hawk moths are perhaps the most distinctive and easily recognized of all the moth families. Their bodies are unusually large and they are strong fliers. Hawk moths can fly at speeds of up to 50km an hour, and many hover like hummingbirds while feeding from flowers. Many hawk moths have very long tongues that enable them to sip nectar from even the deepest flowers. When these moths come to rest, their wings usually angle back like the wings of a jet plane. Hawk moth caterpillars nearly all have a pointed horn on the end of their bodies.

1 Hawk moths begin life as eggs laid on the leaves of a food-plant. The round eggs are a distinctive shiny green. They are laid singly or in small batches and hatch a week or two afterwards.

2 The elephant hawk moth's name comes from the ability of its caterpillar to stretch out its front segments like an elephant's trunk. It takes about six weeks to grow fully and, like most hawk moths, it passes the winter in the pupal stage.

3 The adult elephant hawk moth is one of the prettiest of all moths. It flies for a few weeks in the summer. Its candy-pink wings are a perfect match for the pink garden fuchsias and wild willow-herbs on which it lays its eggs.

Hawk Moths

GOING HUNGRY

During nights in late spring and summer, poplar hawk moths can often be seen flying towards lighted shop windows in European towns. These moths have a short tongue and do not feed as adults. Unusually for hawk moths, when they are resting by day, their hindwings are pushed in front of the forewings.

poplar hawk moth
(*Laothoe populi*)

HONEY LOVER

The death's head hawk moth is named for the skull-like markings near the back of its head. Its proboscis is too short to sip nectar. Instead, it sometimes enters beehives and sucks honey from the combs.

MASTER OF DISGUISE

The broad-bordered bee hawk moth resembles a bumblebee. It has a fat, brown and yellow body and clear, glassy wings. This disguise helps to protect it from predators as it flies during the day.

Spinning Spiders

All spiders make silk. They pull the silk out of spinnerets on their abdomens, usually with their legs. The silk is a syrupy liquid when it first comes out, but pulling makes it harden. The more silk is pulled, the stronger it becomes. Some spider silk is stronger than steel wire of the same thickness. As well as being very strong, silk is incredibly thin, has more stretch than rubber and is stickier than sticky tape. Spiders make up to six different types of silk in different glands in the abdomen. Each type of silk is used for a different purpose, from making webs to wrapping prey. Female spiders produce a special silk to wrap up eggs.

An *Agroeca* spider hangs its cocoon from a grass stem. It will plaster the cocoon with mud to form a hard protective coating.

▲ EGG PARCELS
Female spiders have an extra silk gland for making egg cases called cocoons. These protect the developing eggs.

The Industrious Spider
Spiders have been admired for their tireless spinning for centuries. This picture was painted by the Italian artist Veronese in the 1500s. He wanted to depict the virtues of the great city of Venice, whose wealth was based on trade. To represent hard work and industry he painted this figure of a woman holding up a spider in its web.

▲ A SILKEN RETREAT
Many spiders build silk shelters or nests. The tube-web spider occupies a hole in the bark of a tree. Its tube-shaped retreat has a number of trip lines radiating out like the spokes of a wheel. If an insect trips over a line, the spider rushes out to grab and eat it.

▲ STICKY SILK

Silk oozes out through a spider's spinnerets.
Two or more kinds of silk can be spun at the
same time. Orb-web spiders produce gummy
silk to make their webs sticky.

▲ FOOD PARCEL

A garden spider (*Araneus*) stops a grasshopper
from escaping by wrapping it in silk. The prey
is also paralysed by the spider's poisonous bite.
Most spiders make silk for wrapping prey.

SPINNERETS ▶

A spider's spinnerets
have many fine tubes
on the end. The smaller
tubes, or spools, produce
finer silk for wrapping
prey. Larger tubes,
called spigots, produce
coarser strands for webs.

Spinnerets vary in
size and number.

Spigot — — Spools

Close up of a spinneret.

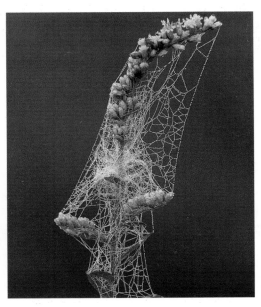

▲ COMBING OUT SILK

This lace-weaver spider is using its back legs
to comb out a special silk. It has an extra
spinning organ (the cribellum) in front of
its spinnerets that produces very fine silk.

▲ VELCRO SILK

The lacy webs made by cribellate spiders
contain tiny loops, like velcro, that catch on
the hairs and bristles of insect prey. Combined
in bands with normal silk, the fluffy-looking
cribellate silk stops insect prey from escaping.

Venom Injection

Nearly all spiders use poison for defence and to kill or paralyse their prey. Spider poison is called venom. It is injected into prey through needle-like jaws called fangs. There are two main kinds of venom that can have serious effects. Most dangerous spiders, such as widow spiders, produce nerve poison to paralyse victims quickly. The other kind of venom works more slowly, destroying tissues and causing ulcers and gangrene. It is made by the recluse spiders. Spider venom is intended to kill insects and small prey — only about 30 spider species are dangerous to people.

▲ VIOLIN SPIDER
This small brown spider is one of the recluse spiders. It lives in people's homes and may crawl into clothes and bedding. Bites from recluse spiders in America have caused ulcers, especially near the wound, and even death in humans.

▲ WANDERING KILLER
The Brazilian wandering spider is a large hunting spider that produces one of the most toxic venoms of all spiders. If disturbed it raises its front legs to expose its threatening jaws. It has the largest venom glands of any spider (up to 10mm long), which hold enough venom to kill 225 mice. Several people have died from this spider's bite.

The Spider Dance
In the Middle Ages people from Taranto in southern Italy called the large wolf spider (Lycosa narbonensis) the tarantula. They believed the venom of this spider's bite could only be flushed from the body by doing the tarantella, a lively dance. However, Lycosa's bite is not serious. An epidemic of dangerous spider bites at the time was probably caused by the malmignatte spider.

▲ SUDDEN DEATH

Crab spiders do not spin webs so they need to kill their prey quickly. They usually inject their venom into the main nerve cords in the neck where the poison will get to work most rapidly. They are able to kill insects much larger than themselves, such as bees.

WIDOW SPIDER ▶

The Australian red-back spider is one of the world's most deadly widow spiders. Widow spiders are named after the female's habit of eating the male after mating. Only female widow spiders are dangerous to people – the much smaller male's fangs are far too tiny to break through human skin.

Did you know? A black widow's venom is 15 times more poisonous than a rattlesnake's.

▲ GENTLE GIANT

Tarantulas look very dangerous and have huge fangs, but at worst their bite is no more painful than a wasp sting. They have small venom glands and are unlikely to bite unless handled roughly. They use venom to digest their prey.

▲ LETHAL BITE

The black widow is a North American spider with venom powerful enough to kill a person (although medicines can now prevent this happening). These shy spiders hide away if disturbed, but like to live near people. One of the main ingredients in their venom knocks out insects and another paralyses mammals and birds by damaging their nervous systems.

145

Stranglers and Poisoners

Most snakes kill their prey before eating it. Snakes kill by using poison or by squeezing their prey to death. Snakes that squeeze are called constrictors and they stop their prey from breathing. Victims die from suffocation or shock. To swallow living or dead prey, a snake opens its jaws wide. Lots of slimy saliva helps the meal to slide down. After eating, a snake yawns widely to put its jaws back into place. Digestion can take several days, or even weeks.

American racer
(Coluber constrictor)

▲ **BIG MOUTHFUL**
This American racer is trying to swallow a living frog. The frog has puffed up its body with air to make it more difficult for the snake to swallow.

▲ **AT FULL STRETCH**
This fer-de-lance snake is at full stretch to swallow its huge meal. It is a large pit viper that kills with poison.

▲ **SWALLOWING A MEAL**
The copperhead, a poisonous snake from North America, holds on to a dead mouse.

▲ KILLING TIME

A crocodile is slowly squeezed to death by a rock python. The time it takes for a constricting snake to kill its prey depends on the size of the prey and how strong it is.

Spotted python
(*Liasis maculosus*)

► COILED KILLER

The spotted python sinks its teeth into its victim. It throws coils around the victim's body, and tightens its grip until the animal cannot breathe.

▼ BREATHING TUBE

An African python shows its breathing tube. As the snake eats, the windpipe moves to the front of the mouth so that air can get to and from the lungs.

▲ HEAD-FIRST

A whiptail wallaby's legs disappear inside a carpet python's body. Snakes usually try to swallow their prey head-first so that legs, wings or scales fold back. This helps the victim to slide into the snake's stomach more easily.

Slithering Scales

▼ POINTED SNOUT

As its name suggests, the European nose-horned viper has a strange horn on its nose. The horn is made up of small scales that lie over a bony or fleshy lump sticking out at the end of the nose.

A snake's scales are extra-thick pieces of skin. Like a suit of armour, the scales protect the snake from knocks and scrapes as it moves. The scales also allow the skin to stretch when the snake moves or feeds. Scales are usually made of a horny substance, called keratin. Every part of a snake's body is covered in scales, even the eyes. Every so often a snake grows a new skin underneath its old one. Then it wriggles out of the dead skin.

Nose-horned viper
(Vipera ammodytes)

▼ SCUTES

Most snakes have a row of broad scales, called scutes, underneath their bodies. The scutes go across a snake's body from side to side, and end where the tail starts. Scutes help snakes to grip the ground.

▼ WARNING RATTLE

The rattlesnake has a number of hollow tail-tips that make a buzzing sound when shaken. The snake uses this sound to warn other animals. When it sheds its skin, a section at the end of the tail is left, adding another piece to the rattle.

Rattlesnake's rattle

Corn snake's scutes

► SKIN SCALES

When a snake's skin is stretched, the scales pull
apart so that you can see the skin between them.
The scales grow out of the top layer of the skin, called the
epidermis. There are different kinds of scales. Smooth scales
make it easier for the snake to squeeze through tight spaces.

*Look closely at the
rough scales of the
puff adder (left) and
you will see a raised
ridge, or keel,
sticking up in the
middle of each one.*

Did you know? Most snakes get their colours from pigments in the scales.

**Corn snake's
scales**

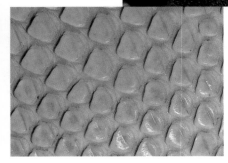

*The wart snake
(right) uses its scales
to grip its food. Its
rough scales help the
snake to keep a firm
hold on slippery fish
until it can swallow
them. The snake's
scales do not overlap.*

*The green scales and
stretched blue skin
(left) belong to a
boa. These smooth
scales help the boa to
slide over leafy
branches. Burrowing
snakes have smooth
scales so that they
can slip through soil.*

Did you know? The hairy bush viper has pointed scales with curled tips, making it look hairy.

Eternal Youth

*A poem written in the Middle East about
3,700 years ago tells a story about why
snakes can shed their skins. The hero of
the poem is Gilgamesh (shown here
holding a captured lion).*

*He finds a
magic plant
that will make
a person young
again. While he
is washing at a
pool, a snake
eats the plant.
Since then,
snakes have
been able to
shed their skins
and become
young again.
But people have
never found the
plant – which
is why they
always grow
old and die.*

Mighty Bites

The huge jaws of a crocodile and its impressive
spiky teeth are lethal weapons for catching prey.
Crocodiles and their relatives (crocodilians) have
two or three times as many teeth as a human.
They have sharp, pointed teeth at the front of the
mouth that are used to pierce and grip prey.
The force of the jaws closing drives these teeth,
like a row of knives, deep into a victim's flesh.
The short, blunt teeth at the back of the mouth
are used for crushing prey. Crocodilian teeth are
no good for chewing food, and the jaws cannot
be moved sideways to chew either. Food has to be
swallowed whole, or torn into chunks. The teeth
are constantly growing. If a tooth falls out, a
new one grows through to replace it.

▲ MEGA JAWS
The jaws of a Nile crocodile
close with tremendous force.
They sink into their prey
with many tonnes of crushing
pressure, but the muscles
that open the jaws are weak.
A thick elastic band over the
snout can easily hold a
crocodile's jaws shut.

◀ NEW TEETH FOR OLD
Each tooth is set in a socket and held in place by a connecting
layer of tissue. Throughout a crocodile's life, the old teeth fall
out and new teeth underneath take their place. Teeth last up
to two years before falling out. Alternate teeth are
replaced together, so that not all the
teeth in one part of the mouth
are lost at once.

◄ LOTS OF TEETH

The gharial has more teeth than any other crocodilian, around 110. Its teeth are also smaller than those of other crocodilians and are all the same size. The narrow, beak-like snout and long, thin teeth of the gharial are geared to grabbing fish with a sweeping sideways movement of the head. The sharp teeth interlock to trap and impale the slippery prey.

CHARMING

Crocodilian teeth are sometimes made into necklaces. People wear them as decoration or lucky charms. In South America, the Montana people of Peru believe they will be protected from poisoning by wearing a crocodile tooth.

▲ BABY TEETH

A baby American alligator is born with a full set of 80 teeth when it hatches from its egg. Baby teeth are not as sharp as adult teeth and are more fragile. They are like tiny needles. In young crocodiles, the teeth at the back of the mouth usually fall out first. In adults it is the teeth at the front that fall out more often.

GRABBING TEETH

A Nile crocodile grasps a lump of prey ready for swallowing. If prey is too large to swallow whole, the crocodile grips the food firmly in its teeth and shakes its head hard so that any unwanted pieces are shaken off.

A Nile crocodile has 68 teeth lining its huge jaws.

Did you know? A Nile crocodile may use 45 sets of teeth by the time it is 4m long.

Cold-blooded Killers

Soon after the sun rises, the first alligators heave themselves out of the river and flop down on the bank. The banks fill up quickly as more alligators join the first, warming their scaly bodies in the sun's rays. As the hours go by and the day gets hotter, the alligators open their toothy jaws wide to cool down. Later in the day, they may go for a swim or crawl into the shade to cool off. As the air chills at night, the alligators slip back into the water again. This is because water stays warmer for longer at night than the land.

Crocodiles and their relatives (crocodilians) are cold-blooded, which means that their body temperature varies with outside temperatures. To warm up or cool down, they move to warm or cool places. Their ideal body temperature is between 30 and 35°C.

▲ **MUD PACK**
A spectacled caiman is buried deep in the mud to keep cool during the hot, dry season. Mud is like water and does not get as hot or as cold as dry land. It also helps to keep the caiman's scaly skin free from bloodsucking parasites.

◄ **SOLAR PANELS**
The crested scutes on the tail of a crocodilian are like the bony plates on armoured dinosaurs. They act like solar panels, picking up heat when the animal basks in the sun. The scutes can also move apart fractionally to let as much heat as possible escape from the body to cool it down.

◄ UNDER THE ICE

An alligator can survive under ice if it keeps a breathing hole open. Of all crocodilians, only alligators stay active at temperatures as low as 12 or 15°C. They do not eat, however, because the temperature is too low for their digestions to work.

▼ OPEN WIDE

While a Nile crocodile suns itself on a rock it also opens its mouth in a wide gape. Gaping helps to prevent the crocodile becoming too hot. The breeze flowing over the wide, wet surfaces of the mouth and tongue dries its moisture and, in turn, cools off its blood. If you lick your finger and blow on it softly, you will notice that it feels a lot cooler.

▲ ALLIGATOR DAYS

Alligators follow a distinct daily routine when the weather is good, moving in and out of the water at regular intervals. If they are disturbed they will also go into the water. In winter, alligators retreat into dens and become sleepy because their blood cools and slows them down.

LESS NEED TO FEED ►

Being cold-blooded can be quite useful. These alligators can bask in the sun without having to eat very much or very often. Warm-blooded animals such as mammals have to eat regularly. They need to eat about five times as much food as crocodilians to keep their bodies warm.

Flying South

Every bird of prey maintains a territory in which it can feed and breed. There is usually no room for the parents' offspring, so they have to forge a new territory themselves. The parents may stay in their breeding area all year long if there is enough food. If not, they may migrate (move away) to somewhere warmer in winter, because sometimes their prey have themselves migrated. For example, peregrines that bred on the tundra in northern Europe fly some 14,000 kilometres to spend winter in South Africa.

EUROPE

ASIA

AFRICA

AUSTRALIA

◄ SOON TIME TO LEAVE
The rough-legged buzzard is slightly larger than its close relative, the common buzzard. It breeds in far northern regions of the world in the spring, both on the treeless tundra and the forested taiga. In the autumn, it migrates south to escape the freezing temperatures of the Arctic winter.

▲ FLIGHT PATHS
Birds avoid migrating over large stretches of water. There are fewer uplifting air currents over water than there are over land. So, many migration routes pass through regions where there is a convenient land bridge or a short sea crossing. Panama, in Central America, is one such area. Gibraltar, in southern Europe, is another.

▼ JUST PASSING THROUGH

This sooty falcon was spotted on its way south to the island of Madagascar, where it spends the winter. In spring, it will return to north-east Africa or Israel to breed.

sooty falcon
(*Falco concolor*)

KEY
→ migration routes of birds of prey

NORTH AMERICA

SOUTH AMERICA

▲ KITE FLYING

The red kite is unmistakable, with its rust-brown belly and white wing patches. There are about 100 red kites in Wales. Unlike many of their European cousins, those that breed in Wales do not usually migrate south in winter.

▲ LONG DISTANCE TRAVELLERS

Graceful kites fly over an Indian village during their annual migration from Asia to warmer winter quarters in southern Africa. They will cover hundreds of kilometres a day.

155

Night Birds

Owls are supreme night hunters with bodies perfectly adapted for hunting in the dark. For one thing, they fly silently. The flight feathers on their wings are covered with a fine down to muffle the sound of air passing over them. Owls' eyes are particularly adapted for night vision. They contain many more rods than the eyes of other bird species. Rods are the structures that make eyes sensitive to light. An owl's hearing is superb too. The rings of fine feathers owls have around their eyes help to channel sounds into the ears. The ears themselves are surrounded by flaps of skin, which can be moved to pinpoint the sources of sounds precisely.

A few other meat-eating birds also hunt after sundown. They include the bat hawk of Africa and Asia, which catches and eats bats and insects while on the wing.

▲ GETTING A GRIP
Like all owls, the barn owl has powerful claws for attacking and gripping prey. The outer toe can be moved backwards and forwards to change grip.

Wise Owls
For centuries, owls have had a reputation for being wise birds. This came about because in Greek mythology, the little owl was the sacred bird of the goddess of wisdom, Athena. She gave her name to Greece's capital city, Athens. The best-known coin of the ancient Greek world was issued in Athens and featured an owl.

▲ GHOSTLY FACE
Of all the owls, the barn owl has the most prominent round face – this is called a facial disc. This gives it a rather ghostly appearance. The disc is formed of short, stiff feathers.

▲ THE WORLD'S LARGEST OWL

A European eagle owl stands over a red fox left out for it as bait. It looks around warily before beginning to eat. The eagle owl is a fierce predator, and will hunt prey as big as a young roe deer. It is a large bird, growing up to 70 cm long, is powerfully built, and has long ear tufts.

▶ OFTEN HEARD, RARELY SEEN

A mouse is carried off by a tawny owl. The long, hooting, 'twit-twoo' call of this owl can be heard in woods, parks and gardens across Europe.

▼ TAKEAWAY MEAL

A barn owl holds on to a mouse it has just caught. Owls usually carry prey in their hooked bills, unlike other birds of prey, which carry it in their claws. Barn owls are found throughout most of the world and in various habitats — moorland, desert, forest and farmland.

barn owl
(*Tyto alba*)

▲ PEEKABOO

A burrowing owl peers out of its nest hole. These small, long-legged birds live in the prairies and grasslands of the New World, from Canada to the tip of South America. They often take over the abandoned holes of other burrowers, such as prairie dogs.

157

Africa's Striped

Vast herds of zebras, gazelles and wildebeest roam the open plains of south and east Africa. They are constantly on the move, searching for better areas of grazing. The herds migrate from the acacia thorn forests in the north-west to the grasslands in the south-east, and back again. Their circular trip takes a year.

Zebras can sense a rainstorm from up to 100km away. They gather into large herds to watch for rain clouds and listen for thunder. The rain fills waterholes and ensures the growth of plenty of fresh, new grass. Zebras are the first to arrive in these areas. They feed on the toughest parts of the vigorous new vegetation, paving the way for the more delicate grazers that follow.

1 From July to September, hundreds of thousands of animals follow the rains from the Serengeti in Tanzania towards the Masai Mara in Kenya. They move in long columns, following the same, well-worn paths every year.

2 One of the major obstacles on the great migration is the Mara River. No animal wants to take the plunge and cross first, as the river is filled with crocodiles. Enormous numbers of zebras and their travelling companions, wildebeest and gazelles, build up on the riverbank.

Migrators

3 When one animal starts to cross, the rest follow quickly. If the river is swollen by the rains, the animals must swim. Some are swept away in the torrent. Smaller members of the herd are pulled down and drowned by crocodiles. If the river is low, the zebras can wade across. They are quite capable of kicking an attacking crocodile with their hind feet and escaping.

4 Lionesses from a resident pride watch and wait among zebra and topi that have crossed the river. They will pounce on any floundering animal. The migrating animals offer a seasonal glut of food as they pass through the lions' territory.

5 The zebras have panicked at the scent of lions nearby and they abandon their river crossing. They will head back on to the plains, regroup and return to the river to try again. Somehow the zebras must cross to get to the new grass on the other side.

6 A lioness chases a scattered herd of zebra and antelope. The pride has fanned out and encircled the herd, chasing them towards an ambush. The migrating animals are followed by hyenas and nomadic lions on the lookout for stragglers and unprotected youngsters.

Trunk Tales

Imagine what it would be like if your nose and top lip were joined together and stretched into a long, bendy tube hanging down from your face. This is what an elephant's trunk must feel like. It can do everything that your nose, lips, hand and arm can do – and more besides. An elephant uses its trunk to breathe, eat, drink, pick things up, throw things, feel, smell, fight and play, squirt water, mud and dust, greet and touch other elephants and make sounds. Not surprisingly, a baby elephant takes a long time to learn all these ways to use its trunk.

▲ DRINKING STRAW

An elephant cannot lower its head down to the ground to drink so it sucks up water with its trunk. Baby elephants drink with their mouths until they learn to use their trunks to squirt water into their mouths.

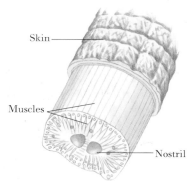

Skin

Muscles

Nostril

▲ A CLOSER LOOK

The two holes in the centre of the trunk are nostrils, through which the elephant breathes. Thousands of muscles pull against each other in different directions to move the trunk.

▲ WEIGHT LIFTER

An African elephant coils its trunk around a branch to lift it off the ground. Elephants can lift whole tree trunks in this way. The powerful trunk has more than 100,000 muscles, which enable an elephant to lift large, heavy objects easily.

▲ TAKING A SHOWER

An elephant does not need to stand under a shower to be sprayed with water, mud or dust. Its trunk is like a built-in shower, able to cover almost its whole body as it reaches backwards over the head. Showering cools the elephant down and gets rid of insects.

▲ BENDY APPENDAGE

Elephants sometimes double up their trunks and rest them on their tusks. They can do this because the trunk has no bones inside it, just muscles, which makes it very flexible.

► TALL ORDER

African elephants use their long, stretchy trunks to pull leaves off the branches of tall acacia trees. The highest leaves are the most juicy. The trunk is slightly telescopic, which means that, if necessary, it can be stretched out even longer than usual. The trunk can also be pushed into small holes or gaps between rocks to find hidden pools of water.

Asian elephant

African elephant

▲ IDENTIFYING TIPS

The trunk of an African elephant has two fingers at the tip, while the Asian elephant has only one. These fingers can pick up an object as small as a leaf or a coin.

Jumbo

Elephants love water. They drink lots of it and enjoy going into lakes and rivers to play and splash around. Elephants are good swimmers and can easily cross rivers or swim out to sea to reach islands with fresh food. They drink at least once a day, or more often when water is available. When water is hard to find in the wild, elephants can be very sneaky, drinking from taps, pipes or water tanks. This usually causes damaged or broken pipes. Elephants can go without water for up to two weeks.

SPLASHING ABOUT

Elephants spray each other with water, wrestle with their trunks and flop sideways with great splashes. Sometimes they turn upside down and poke the soles of their feet out of the water. All this play strengthens the bonds between individuals and keeps groups together.

LIQUID REFRESHMENT

These two elephants are refreshing themselves at a waterhole. Elephants drink by sucking in water through their trunk. They seal off the end with the finger or fingers at the end of the trunk. Then they lift the trunk to the mouth and squirt in the water.

CHAMPION SWIMMERS

Elephants are good at swimming even though they are so big. When an elephant swims underwater, it pokes its trunk above the water and uses it like a snorkel to breathe through.

Water Babies

KEEPING CLEAN
Frequent bathing washes the build-up of mud and dust out of the cracks in an elephant's thick skin. Disease-carrying insects and parasites that feed off the elephant's skin are also washed off in the water.

HOLDING ON TIGHT
In the water, baby elephants often hold on to the tail of the elephant in front for safety. They can easily be swept away by fast-flowing rivers. Baby elephants are also vulnerable to attack from crocodiles.

THIRST QUENCHER
An elephant needs to drink 70–90 litres of water a day. A full trunk of water holds about 5–10 litres. Incredibly, a very thirsty adult elephant can drink about 100 litres of water in 5 minutes.

163

Great Navigators

Bears have an uncanny knack of finding their way home even in unfamiliar territory. How they do this is only just beginning to be understood. For long distances, they rely on an ability to detect the Earth's magnetic field. This provides them with a magnetic map of their world and a compass to find their way around. When closer to home, they recognize familiar landmarks. In fact, bears have extraordinary memories, especially where food is involved. For example, a mother and her cubs are known to have trekked 32km to a favourite oak tree to feast on acorns. Five years later, the same cubs (now adults) were reported to have been seen at the same tree.

Stars in the Sky
The Great Bear constellation in the northern hemisphere is known to astronomers as Ursa Major. In Greek mythology, it was said to have been made in the shape of a she-bear and placed in the heavens by Zeus. The Great Bear is also worshipped in Hindu mythology as the power that keeps the heavens turning. The Inuit believe these stars represent a bear being continually chased by dogs.

▲ **ARCTIC NOMADS**
Polar bears are capable of swimming long distances between ice floes, at speeds of up to 10km/h. They may travel thousands of kilometres across the frozen Arctic Ocean and the surrounding lands in search of prey.

▲ **BAD BEAR**
A sedated polar bear is transported a safe distance out of town. Nuisance bears are often moved this way but they unerringly find their way back.

◀ TO AND FROM THE FOREST

The polar bears of Hudson Bay, Canada, migrate to the forests in summer and return to hunt on the sea ice in winter. On their return journey, they sometimes stop off at the town of Churchill. They gather at the rubbish tip there to feed on leftovers, while they wait for ice to reform.

KEY

 Bears return to ice in winter

 Bears come ashore in June and July

 Bears walk north in autumn

▲ REGULAR ROUTES

Polar bears move quickly even on fast, shifting ice floes. A bear moving north, for example, against the southward-drifting ice in the Greenland Sea, can travel up to 80km in a day.

▲ RELYING ON MEMORY

Male brown bears live in large home ranges covering several hundred square kilometres. They must remember the locations of food and the different times of year it is available.

The Big Sleep

Black bears, brown bears and pregnant female polar bears sleep during the winter months. They do this because food is scarce, not because of the cold. Scientists have argued for years about whether bears truly hibernate or merely doze during the winter months and this argument still goes on today. During this sleep, or hibernation, a brown bear's heart rate drops to about 10 beats per minute. American black bears reduce their blood temperature by at least one degree. They do not eat or drink for up to four months. Bears survive only on the fat that they have stored during the summer months. A bear might lose up to half its body-weight before it awakes at the end of the winter.

▲ FAT BEAR

Before the winter sleep a bear can become quite tubby. Fat reserves make up more than half of this black bear's body-weight. It needs this bulk to make sure that it has enough fat on its body to survive the winter fast. In the weeks leading up to the winter, a bear must consume large quantities of energy-rich foods, such as salmon.

Did you know? Some hibernating bears sleep for 5½ months non-stop.

◄ HOME COMFORTS

A brown bear pulls in grass and leaves to cushion its winter den. American black bears and brown bears sleep in small, specially dug dens. These are usually found on the sunny, south-facing slopes of mountains.

▲ **FOREST REFUGE**

A hole dug by a brown bear serves as its winter den in this Swedish forest. Bears spend winter in much stranger places, such as under cabins occupied by people, beneath bridges or beside busy roads.

▲ **READY FOR ACTION**

If disturbed, a bear wakes easily from its winter sleep. Although it is dormant, a bear's body is ready to be active. It is able to defend itself immediately against predators, such as a hungry wolf pack.

▲ **SNOW HOUSE**

Female polar bears leave the drifting ice floes in early winter and head inland to excavate a nursery den. They dig deep down into the snow and ice, tunnelling for about 5m to make the den. Here they will give birth to their cubs. In severe weather, male polar bears rest by lying down and allowing themselves to be covered over by an insulating layer of snow.

▲ **WINTER NURSERY**

In the early winter, one bear enters a den, but three might emerge in spring. Female polar bears, like most bears, give birth while hidden away in their dens. The tiny cubs (usually twins) are born in the middle of winter, in December or January.

Camouflaged Cats

A cat's fur coat protects its skin and keeps it warm. The coat's colours and patterns help to camouflage (hide) the cat as it hunts prey. Wild cats' coats have two layers – an undercoat of short soft fur and an outercoat of tougher, longer hairs, called guard hairs. Together these two layers insulate the cat from extreme cold or extreme heat. Some guard hairs are sensitive and help a cat to feel its way. Cats have loose skin, making it hard for an attacker to get a good grip and helping to prevent injury. The colours and patterns of a wild cat's coat depend on where it lives.

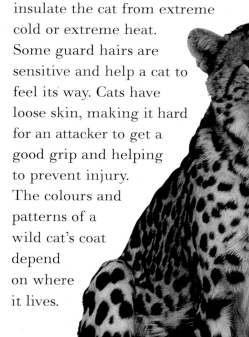

▲ **TIGER IN THE GRASS**
The stripes of a tiger's coat are the perfect camouflage for an animal that needs to prowl around in long grass. The colours and patterns help to make the cat almost invisible as it stalks its prey. These markings are also very effective in a leafy jungle where the dappled light makes stripes of light and shade.

Did you know? Domestic cats have a wider range of colours and markings than wild cats.

◀ **KING OF THE HILL**
King cheetahs were once thought to be different from other cheetahs. They have longer fur, darker colours and spots on their backs that join up to form stripes. Even so, they are the same species. All cheetahs have distinctive tear stripes running from the corners of their eyes down beside their muzzles.

▲ NON-IDENTICAL TWINS

Many big cats of the same species come in variations of colour, depending on where they live. These two leopard cubs are twins, but one has a much darker, blackish coat. Black leopards are called panthers. (Black jaguars and even pumas are sometimes called panthers.) Some leopards live deep in the shadows of the forest, where darker colouring allows them to hide more easily. Panthers are most common in Asia.

▼ SPOT THE DIFFERENCE

Spots, stripes or blotches break up the outline of a cat's body. This helps it to blend in with the shadows made by the leaves of bushes and trees, or the lines of tall grass. In the dappled light of a forest or in the long grass of the savanna, cats are very well hidden indeed.

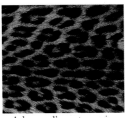

A leopard's spots are in fact small rosettes.

The tiger has distinctive black stripes.

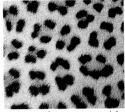

A jaguar has rosettes with a central spot of colour.

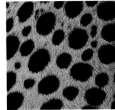

The cheetah has lots of spots and no rosettes.

◄ MOUNTAIN DWELLER

A snow leopard has a shaggy, off-white coat with darker spots. This colouring helps the snow leopard to stay well hidden in the rocky, mountainous terrain where it lives. It moves around early in the morning or late in the afternoon, blending with its habitat as it looks for prey.

A snow leopard's pale, thick coat has dark irregular spots and streaks. This helps the cat to hide between the rocks and snow.

169

The Dry Life

Deserts are very dry places. Although most are hot during the day, at night they are very cold. Few plants and animals can survive in such a harsh environment, but cats are very adaptable. Cheetahs, lions and leopards live in the Kalahari and Namib deserts of southern Africa. As long as there are animals to eat, the cats can survive. Even the jaguar, a cat that loves water, has been seen in desert areas in Mexico and the southern USA. But they are only visitors in this tough, dry land and soon go back to the wetter places they prefer. The best adapted cat to desert life is a small species known as the sand cat. It lives in the northern Sahara Desert, the Middle East and western Asia.

Did you know? Lions travel along dry riverbeds looking for waterholes in the desert.

▲ **DESERT STORM**
Two lions endure a sandstorm in the Kalahari Desert of southern Africa. The desert is a very hostile place to live. There is very little water, not much food and the wind blows up terrible sandstorms. Despite these hardships, big cats like these lions manage to survive.

This map shows where the world's hot deserts and nearby semi-desert areas are located.

▼ **A HARSH LIFE**
An old lion drinks from a waterhole in the Kalahari Desert. Even when a big cat lives in a dry place, it still needs to find enough water to drink. This is often a difficult task, requiring the animals to walk long distances. In the desert, prey is usually very spread out, so an old lion has a hard time trying to feed itself adequately.

▲ CHEETAH WALK

A group of cheetahs walk across the wide expanse of the Kalahari Desert. They lead lives of feast and famine. In the rainy season, some vegetation grows and herds of antelope can graze. The cheetahs have a banquet preying on the grazing herds. But they go very hungry as the land dries up and prey becomes scarce.

Big ears hear the soft, high-pitched squeaks of rodents.

◄ SAND CAT

Dense hair on the pads of the sand cat's feet protect it as it stands on hot ground and help it to walk on loose sand. All the water the cat needs comes from its food, so it does not need to drink.

Very thick, soft fur protects from the heat and cold.

▲ ADAPTABLE LEOPARD

A leopard rolls in the desert sand. There are very few trees in the desert, so leopards live among rocky outcrops. Here they can drag their prey to high places to eat in safety. The desert can be a dangerous place. With so little food around, competition can be fierce, especially with hungry lions. Big cats will eat small prey such as insects to keep from starving.

Egyptian Cat Worship
The Ancient Egyptians kept cats to protect their stores of grain from rats and mice. Cats became so celebrated that they were worshipped as gods. They were sacred to the cat-headed goddess of pleasure, Bast. Many cats were given funerals when they died. Their bodies were preserved, wrapped in bandages and richly painted.

Fur Coats

black-backed jackal
(Canis mesomelas)

Wolves and other members of the dog family have thick fur coats. This dense layer of hair helps to protect the animal's body from injury and keeps it warm in cold weather. Wolves and other dogs that live in cold places have extra-thick fur. Dingoes, jackals and wild dogs that live in warm countries close to the equator have sparser fur. The fur is made up of two layers. Short dense underfur helps to keep the animal warm. Long guard hairs on top have natural oils that repel snow and rain to keep the underfur dry. A wild dog's fur coat is usually black, white or tan, or a mixture of these. Markings and patterns on the fur act as camouflage to disguise these animals, so they can sneak up on their prey.

▲ DISTINCTIVE OUTFIT

The three species of jackal can be distinguished by their different markings. As its name suggests, the black-backed jackal has a dark patch on its back as well as brown flanks and a pale belly. The golden jackal is sandy brown all over. The side-striped jackal is so named because of the light and dark stripes that run along its sides.

◄ WRAPPED UP WARM

Two raccoon dogs shelter under a bush at the end of winter. Raccoon dogs are the only dogs in the world to hibernate. Their thick fur helps them survive through their long winter sleep. Originally from east Asia, raccoon dogs were brought to western Russia by fur farmers in the 1920s. Some escaped and they can now be found in eastern Europe.

◄ MANES AND RUFFS

The maned wolf gets its name from the ruff of long hairs on its neck. This may be dark or reddish brown in colour. Wolves also have a ruff of longer hairs that they raise when threatened, to make themselves look larger.

▲ HANDSOME CAMOUFLAGE

African hunting dogs have beautiful markings, with tan and dark grey patches on their bodies, and paler, mottled fur on their heads and legs. The patterns work to break up the outline of their bodies as they hunt in the dappled light of the bush.

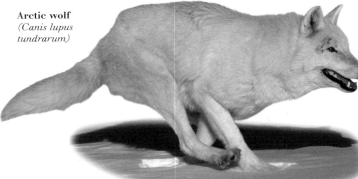

Arctic wolf
(Canis lupus tundrarum)

▲ ICE WHITE

The Arctic wolf has very thick fur to keep it warm in icy temperatures. Its winter coat is pure white so that it blends in with the snow. In spring, the thick fur drops out and the wolf grows a thinner coat for summer. This coat is usually darker to match the earth without its covering of snow.

VARYING COLOURS ►

Grey wolves vary greatly in colour, from pale silver to buff, sandy, red-brown or almost black. Even very dark wolves usually have some pale fur, often a white patch on the chest.

grey wolf
(Canis lupus)

Snow Dogs

Wolves were once widespread throughout the northern hemisphere. As human settlements have expanded, so wolves have been confined to more remote areas such as the far north. The Arctic is a frozen wilderness where very few people live. Wolves and Arctic foxes are found here. On the barren, treeless plains known as the tundra, harsh, freezing winter weather lasts for nine months of the year. Both land and sea are buried beneath a thick layer of snow and ice. Few animals are active in winter, so prey is scarce. During the brief summer, the ice and snow melt, flowers bloom and birds, insects and animals flourish, so prey is abundant. Arctic wolves and foxes rear their cubs in this time of plenty. Another harsh, remote habitat, the windswept grass steppes of Asia, is home to the small steppe wolf.

Arctic Legend
Native Americans named natural phenomena after the animals that lived around them. The Blackfoot people called the Milky Way the Wolf Trail. In Canada, the Cree believed the Northern Lights, shown below, shone when heavenly wolves visited the Earth. In fact these spectacular light shows in the Arctic are caused by particles from the Sun striking the Earth's atmosphere.

◄ POLAR GIANT
Arctic wolves are larger than most other wolves. They scrape under the snow to nibble plant buds and lichen if they are desperate for food.

Arctic wolf
(Canis lupus tundrarum)

Did you know? The largest Arctic wolf territories cover 13,000 sq km—an area about the same size as Northern Ireland.

▲ COSY HOOD

This Inuit girl is wearing a hood trimmed with wolf fur. The fur is warm and sheds the ice that forms on the hood's edge as the wearer breathes. The Inuit and other peoples of the far north traditionally dressed in the skins of Arctic animals. Animal skins make the warmest clothing and help to camouflage the wearer when hunting.

▲ NORTHERN HUNTER

A grey wolf feeds hungrily on a caribou carcass. In the icy north, wolves need very large territories to find enough prey. They will follow deer for hundreds of kilometres as the herds move south for the winter.

◄ ARCTIC HELPERS

One crack of a whip brings a team of huskies under control. Tough and hardy huskies, with their thick fur coats, are working dogs of the far north. They are used by the Inuit and other Arctic peoples to pull sleds and to help in hunting.

SNOWY BED ►

A grey wolf shelters in a snowy hollow to escape a howling blizzard. With its thick fur, it can sleep out in the open in temperatures as low as -46°C. Snow drifting over its body forms a protective blanket.

Monkey Magic

Primates are the most versatile movers of the animal world. Many can walk and run, climb and swim. Small monkeys and the larger lemurs can leap between branches. This method is risky for larger animals, in case a branch breaks beneath their weight. Heavier primates play safe by walking along branches on all fours and avoid jumping if possible.

When branches are bendy, climbers move with caution. They may use their weight to swing from one handhold to the next, but they do not let go of one handhold until the other is in place. Tree-climbing monkeys have long fingers to curl around branches and help them to grip.

Monkeys that live on the ground use their hands as well as their feet to propel themselves along.

Did you know? A spider monkey's tail is so strong it can support the monkey's entire weight.

spider monkey
(*Ateles geoffroyanus*)

◄ **HANGING AROUND**
New World monkeys rarely move at ground level. Most swing from tree to tree, stop and whip their tail around a branch, let go with both hands and grab something to eat. Old World monkeys do not have a prehensile (grasping) tail. Many have very short tails or no tail at all.

◄ **PADDED MITTS**
The palm of a sifaka lemur is one of the features that makes it a star jumper. The wrinkles and fleshy pads are like a baseball glove, giving extra holding power. Sifakas can push off with their long hind legs to leap up to 5m high. Their arms are short, making it impossible to walk on all fours. Instead, sifakas hop on both feet.

◀ BABOONS ON THE MOVE

A troop of baboons makes its way down a track in the African savanna. They are strong and tough because they have to walk long distances to find enough food to feed the troop. Baboons and other monkeys that walk on the ground, such as mandrills, geladas and macaques, put their weight on the fingertips and palms of their hands and feet. This is different from apes, such as gorillas and chimpanzees, who walk on their knuckles.

LIGHT AS AIR ▶

A pygmy marmoset can perch on the flimsiest of twigs. It has to be small, light and quick to catch the insects that it eats. Marmosets scurry along branches rather like squirrels, and for this reason are the only primates to have claws instead of nails. They are also able to sit up on their hind legs to free their hands for collecting food as well as for feeding.

▲ SLOW AND STEADY

Lorises from Sri Lanka and southern India are known for their slow, deliberate movements. They have long, thin arms and legs with very flexible ankles and wrists. A loris can wriggle its way through, and get a grip on, dense twigs and small branches. Due to its strange appearance, some people describe the animal as a banana on stilts.

177

Hands and Feet

Can you imagine how difficult it would be to pick something up if your arms ended in paws, hooves or flippers? It would be impossible to grip any object and you could not turn it around, carry it, throw it, pull it apart or put it together. An ape's hands and feet are remarkable. They are very adaptable, and the opposable thumb or big toe enables them to grasp firmly or hold delicately. Ape hands and feet are strong and flexible, allowing apes to climb, swing and jump through the treetops. They also allow apes to reach food, investigate their surroundings, groom their family and friends and build nests. In most apes, the feet look very much like hands, but in humans, the feet look different. This is because human feet are adapted for walking rather than climbing.

▲ **SMILE PLEASE**
Grasping a delicate camera lens, a gorilla demonstrates how it can pick up fragile objects without breaking them. A gorilla has thicker, sturdier hands than a person, with fingers the size of bananas and a smaller thumb. Its hands have to be strong so that they can support the weight of the gorilla's body when it walks around on all fours.

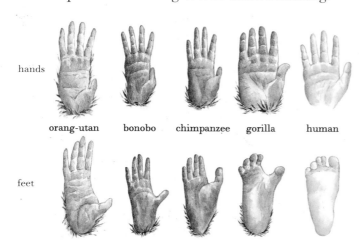

hands

orang-utan   bonobo   chimpanzee   gorilla   human

feet

◄ **LOOK-ALIKE HANDS**
The hands of the great apes have several features in common, such as nails and long, sensitive fingers. The thumb on a great ape's hand goes off at an angle and can press against each finger. The big toe on an ape's foot can also do this, except in humans. Bonobos have a unique feature not shared by the other apes — webbing between the second and third toes.

Did you know?
5 million hairs on their bodies.
Humans have over

orang-utan
(Pongo pygmaeus)

▲ OPPOSABLE THUMB

Since a great ape's thumb can easily touch, or oppose, its fingers, it is called an opposable thumb. This special thumb gives an ape's hand a precise pincer grip, allowing it to pick up objects as small as berries.

▲ GRAPPLING IRONS

An orang-utan's arms and legs end in huge hands and feet that work like powerful clamps. Just one hand or foot can take the entire weight of the ape.

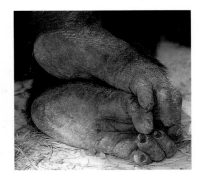

▲ HAND-FOOT

Unlike a human, a chimp can use its feet rather like hands, to hold and investigate things. The opposable big toe stretches out around one side of a branch while the other toes reach around the other side, giving a very strong grip.

▲ FLAT FEET

Chimpanzees are flat-footed, with tough, hairless soles and long toes. When upright, their feet have to take all of the body weight.

Chimps

Humans were once thought to be the only animals clever enough to use tools. Now we know that a handful of other animals, such as Galapagos finches and sea otters, use them too. However, these animals are only beginners compared to chimpanzees. A chimp chooses its tools, changes them to make them better and uses them over and over again. Chimps plan ahead, collecting sticks or stones on their way to a source of food. Their nimble fingers and creative minds help them to invent and use tools. Adult chimps are good at concentrating, sometimes spending hours using their tools.

MAKING A TOOL
This chimpanzee is shaping a stick to help her dig for food. Chimpanzees have invented several clever ways to use sticks.

TASTY SNACKS
An intelligent chimp can shape and manipulate a grass stem to form a useful tool for fishing out termites from a mound. Scientists who have tried to copy the chimps have found that termite fishing is much, much harder than it looks.

FISHING FOR FOOD
This captive chimp is using a stick, in the same way as a chimp in the wild would use a grass stem, to fish in a termite mound. However, the termite mound in the zoo probably has yogurt or honey inside it, rather than termites.

That Use Tools

LEAF SPONGE

A wodge of leaves makes a useful sponge to soak up rainwater from tree holes. Chewing the leaf first breaks up its waterproof coating, so that it soaks up more water. Leaves may also be used as toilet paper, to wipe blood from wounds and to scrape up sticky food.

HANDY WEAPON

Wild chimps can only make tools from objects in their environment, which is why sticks are so important. Sticks make good weapons for attack and defence. They can also be used as levers, and thin sticks make a natural dental floss.

CRACKING PERFORMANCE

In West Africa, chimps use hammers and anvils to crack open the hard shells of nuts. Hammers are made from logs or stones, anvils from stones or tree roots. Hammer stones can weigh as much as 20kg. A skilled adult can crack a shell with just a few blows.

Underwater Voices

Sounds travel easily in water. Whales use
sounds to communicate with one another and
to find their food. The baleen (filter-feeding)
whales use low-pitched sounds, which have
been picked up by underwater microphones as
moans, grunts and snores. Dolphins and most
other toothed whales communicate and hunt
using higher-pitched clicks. They send out
beams of sounds, which are reflected by objects,
such as fish. The dolphin picks up the reflected
sound, or echo, and can work out where
the object is. This is called
echo-location.

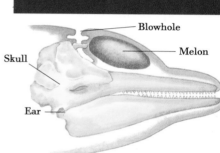

Blowhole

Melon

Skull

Ear

◄ ECHO SOUNDINGS
The Amazon river dolphin,
or boto, hunts by echo-
location. It sends out high-
pitched clicking sounds, up
to 80 clicks every second.
The sound is transmitted in
a broad beam from a bulge,
called a melon, on top of its head.

► SEA CANARIES
A group of belugas, or white whales,
swims in a bay in Canada. Belugas'
voices can clearly be heard above the
surface. This is why they are known
as sea canaries. They also produce
high-pitched sounds we cannot hear,
which they use for echo-location.

▲ MAKING WAVES
A dolphin makes high-pitched sound
waves by vibrating the air in the
passages in its nose. The waves are
focused into a beam by the melon. The
sound is transmitted into the water.

◄ SUPER SONGSTER

This male humpback whale is heading
for the breeding grounds where the
females are gathering. The male starts
singing long and complicated songs.
This may be to attract a mate or to
warn other males off its patch. The
sound can carry for 30km or more.

▼ WATER MUSIC

This is a voice print of a humpback
whale's song, picked up by an
underwater microphone. It shows
complex musical phrases and
melodies. Humpback whales often
continue singing for a day or more,
repeating the same song.

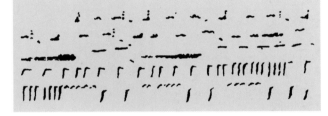

▼

**SOUND
ECHOES**

A sperm whale
can locate a giant
squid more than a
kilometre away by
transmitting pulses of sound
waves into the water and
listening. The echo is picked up
by the teeth in its lower jaw and
the vibrations are sent
along the jaw to the ear.

Did you know?
A dolphin picks up sounds through its lower jaw.

◄ ALIEN GREETINGS

The songs of the humpback
whale not only travel through
Earth's oceans, but they are also
travelling far out into Space.
They are among the recorded
typical sounds of our world that
are being carried by the two Voyager space
probes. These probes are now millions of
kilometres away from Earth and are on
their way far beyond our solar system.

frilled shark
(Chlamydoselachus anguineus)

Deep-sea Sharks

Many sharks are rarely seen because they live in the darkness of the deep. Catsharks and dogfish live in these gloomy waters, glowing in the dark with a luminous green-blue or white light. Some of these species travel and hunt in packs, following their prey to the surface at night and returning into the depths by day. Most of the world's smallest sharks live in the deep sea. Pygmy and dwarf sharks no bigger than a cigar travel for several kilometres through the ocean each day. On the deep-sea floor are enormous sharks such as the sixgill, sevengill and sleeper sharks. These eat the remains of dead animals that sink down from the sea's surface. Many deep-sea sharks look primitive, but strangest of all are the frilled and horned goblin sharks. These look like the fossilized sharks that swam the seas 150 million years ago.

▲ LIVING FOSSIL

The frilled shark is the only shark shaped like an eel. It has six feathery gill slits, 300 tiny, three-pointed teeth and a large pair of eyes. Like all sharks, it has a skeleton of flexible cartilage. These features show that the frilled shark resembles fossilized species that lived in the oceans millions of years ago.

▲ DEEP-SEA TRAVELLER

The shortnose spurdog can be recognized by a spine at the front of each dorsal fin. It lives in packs made up of thousands of sharks. It swims at depths of 800m in the northern waters of the Pacific and Atlantic oceans. At certain times of the year, the packs make a daily migration, from north to south and from coastal to deeper waters.

shortnose spurdog
(Squalus megalops)

▼ DEEPEST OF THE DEEP

The Portuguese dogfish holds the shark record for living in the deepest waters. One was caught 2,718m below the sea's surface. At this depth, the water temperature is no higher than a chilly 5–6°C.

Portuguese dogfish
(Centroscymnus coelolepis)

◄ SIX GILL SLITS

Most modern sharks have five gill slits, but primitive sharks, such as this bluntnose sixgill shark, have more. These species are found at huge depths around the world. They have evolved (developed) slowly, and still have the features of sharks that lived millions of years ago.

▼ SEVEN GILL SLITS

Broadnose sevengill sharks have seven gill slits. They have primitive, sharp teeth that look like tiny combs. They use these to slice up ratfish, small sharks and mackerel. Because some of their prey live near the surface, sevengill sharks travel up to the sea's surface to hunt at night.

broadnose sevengill shark
(*Notorynchus cepedianus*)

Did you know? Many deep-sea sharks have light organs on their bodies.

velvet belly
(*Etmopterus spinax*)

◄ SLIMY COAT

The velvet belly is 66cm long. It lives in the Atlantic and Mediterranean at depths of 70–2,000m. The velvet belly is covered with luminous slime, and the underside of its body has special organs that give out light. It eats deep-sea fish and shrimps.

185

Attack of

1 Huge groups of albatrosses nest on the ground close to the shore of Hawaiian islands, including the island of Laysan. The birds in each group breed, nest, and hatch their babies at the same time. When it is time, the young birds all take their first flight within days of each other.

Sharks can be found wherever there is food in or near the sea. Tiger sharks are rarely seen around some of the Hawaiian islands in the Pacific Ocean, but when the islands' young seabirds start to fly the sharks arrive suddenly. Any birds that fall into the sea are quickly eaten. The waters are too shallow for the tiger sharks to attack from behind and below as most sharks do. Instead, the sharks leap clear of the surface then drag the birds underwater to drown and eat them. Sharks arrive for their island feast at the same time each year. How they remember to do so is yet to be explained.

2 When ready to fly, a baby albatross practises by flapping its wings in the face of the islands' fierce winds. Eventually, the baby must make its first real flight over the ocean. When it does so, the tiger sharks are waiting in the water below.

3 Tiger sharks patrol the clear, shallow waters close to the albatross nests. Their dark shapes can be seen clearly against the sandy sea floor. Every now and again, a tiger shark's triangular dorsal fin and the tip of its tail can be seen breaking the water's surface.

the Tiger Sharks

4 Any baby bird that dips into the sea is prey for the waiting tiger shark. At first, the shark tries its usual attack, from below and behind. However, in the shallow waters the shark cannot make a full attack. Rather than hitting its prey at force, the shark just pushes the bird away on the wave made by its snout.

5 After failing to catch a meal, the shark soon realizes its mistake and tries another approach. Its next style of attack is to shoot across the surface of the water, slamming into its target with its mouth wide open. This technique seems to be more successful, and the shark usually catches the bird.

6 The shark then attempts to drag the bird below the surface, to drown it. If a bird is pushed ahead on the shark's bow wave, it will bravely peck at its attacker's broad snout and sometimes may even escape. Some birds also manage to wriggle free as the shark grapples with them underwater.

7 Many albatross babies do not manage to escape a shark attack. They are grabbed by the sharks and drowned. Inside the tiger shark's jaws are rows of sharp teeth that can slice into a bird's body like a saw. Sometimes the tiger shark tears off the bird's wings and leaves them aside to eat the body whole.

Animals in Danger

Changes in climate or living conditions have caused some animal species to die out. More recently people have interfered with nature, endangering the future of many animals. This section examines why animals are in danger of becoming extinct and what is being done to protect them.

Facing Extinction

Over 6,000,000,000 people are living on the earth today, and numbers are growing at the rate of nearly 80,000,000 every year. Every day we take up more land for houses and crops as well as roads and factories, so there is less room for wildlife. The only animals that benefit from the human population explosion are things like cabbage white butterflies, grain weevils, and carpet beetles that have become pests on our crops and in our homes.

Habitat Destruction

The greatest threat to the world's wildlife is the loss of habitat. Rainforests are being destroyed at an alarming rate – in some parts of the world over 30 hectares are being cut down every minute – and with them go all the plants and animals that lived there. Scientists have estimated that about 50 species of rainforest plants and animals disappear every day. Thousands more species are in danger of becoming extinct in the next few years. They include the tiger, the Philippine eagle, and many beautiful butterflies. Elsewhere in the world, wetlands are being drained and grasslands are being ploughed up for crops or covered with concrete. Pollution of the air and the water harms many more animals, and so does the widespread use of insecticides and weedkillers.

Hunted for Food and Fun

People who traditionally hunted animals for food with bows and arrows did no harm to the wildlife populations. The invention of high-powered rifles, harpoons and other deadly weapons,

Dolphins and killer whales are always popular animals at aquariums, but it is not to their benefit to keep them in captivity.

however, meant that large numbers of animals could be killed for 'sport' and for skins, or simply because they competed with domestic livestock. Many animals then became rare and further hunting of them has put them in even greater danger.

Fishing is also a serious threat to some animals; the fishing nets that are now being used to catch tuna and other seawater fishes also kill large numbers of dolphins. The animals get tangled up in the nets and are unable to get to the surface to breathe. Conservationists are urging people not to buy the fish that are caught by these killer nets in an attempt to prevent the problem.

The Remedies

The most obvious and important thing is to stop destroying wild habitats. Many animals are already protected in nature reserves, where the habitats are safe from destruction, but before creating reserves biologists need to know how much space the animals need and how far they travel in their search for food. Such information is often obtained by putting little radio transmitters on the animals and listening for the signals to find out where the animals go. This has been done with bears, wolves, and big cats.

Many countries have laws that control hunting and prohibit the killing of rare and endangered animals, but it is not easy to enforce these laws because it is impossible to patrol vast areas of forest and savanna. Elephants and big cats are legally protected but poachers still kill them for their ivory and skins. The Convention on International Trade in Endangered Species (CITES) is dedicated to stopping all trade in endangered species and any

Gorillas, orang-utans, chimpanzees and bonobos are all endangered species. To help them survive in the future, their habitat needs to be protected in national parks or reserves.

article that comes from them – such as ivory, tortoiseshell, skins, fur and feathers. If the objects cannot be exported or sold, people will hopefully be less interested in killing the animals.

Re-introductions

Several species that have been threatened with extinction have been saved by being taken into zoos or wildlife parks and bred there in safety. When the population is big enough, it is sometimes

possible to release the animals back into the wild – as long as suitable habitat remains or can be re-created. The Arabian oryx was the first large animal to be saved from extinction in this way. Other animals that have been successfully re-established in the wild include the Hawaiian goose, Przewalski's horse, and the golden lion tamarin.

Many species of wild horses and asses are a cause for concern as they live in isolated groups and are in great danger of becoming extinct.

A bright outlook?

The future for some wild animals depends on whether their habitat can remain, if they continue to be destroyed then the only place that these large and fascinating animals will be seen will be in the confined spaces of zoos.

Battling Beetles and Bugs

Beetles and bugs do many jobs that benefit people, either directly or indirectly. They pollinate plants and consume waste matter. They are also a valuable food source for other animals, including reptiles and birds.

However, most people regard these insects as pests because they can harm us or our lands and possessions. Aphids, chafers and weevils attack crop-fields, orchards, vegetable plots and gardens. Wood-boring beetles damage timber and furniture, and other beetles attack carpets and clothes. Blood-sucking bugs spread many human and livestock diseases, while sap-sucking bugs may carry plant diseases. People wage war against these pests – and many other harmless beetles and bugs. Some species are in danger of dying out altogether because people are killing them, or destroying the places in which they live.

▲ CARPET-CRUNCHER
A carpet beetle larva munches on a woollen carpet. These young beetles become pests when they hatch out on carpets and clothes. The larvae have spines on their bodies that protect them from enemies. A close relative, the museum beetle, also causes havoc. It eats its way through preserved animal specimens in museums.

COLLECTING INSECTS ▶
If you are collecting insects, remember to handle them carefully so that you do not damage them. Always return insects to the place where you found them. Do not try to catch delicate insects such as dragonflies, or ones that could sting you, such as wasps.

▲ DUTCH ELM DISEASE

Elm bark beetles are wood-borers. The fungus they carry causes Dutch elm disease, which kills elm trees. During the 1970s, a major outbreak of the disease destroyed most of the elm trees in Britain.

Manna from Heaven
The Old Testament of the Bible tells how the ancient Israelites survived in the desert by eating 'manna'. After many centuries of debate, historians now believe this strange food may have been scale insects, living on tamarisk trees.

▲ WOODWORM DAMAGE

This chair has fallen prey to woodworm. These beetles can literally reduce wood to powder. Laid as eggs inside the timber, the young feed on the wood until they are ready to pupate. As winged adults, they quickly bore their way to freedom, leaving tell-tale exit holes in the wood.

▲ GARDENERS' FRIEND

These black bean aphids are infested with tiny parasitic wasps. The female wasp lays her eggs on the aphids. When the young hatch, they eat the bugs. Gardeners consider aphids to be pests and welcome the wasps in their gardens. Wasps are sometimes used in large numbers by gardeners to control pests.

Swarms and Armies

Social insects affect our lives and the world we live in. We think of some species as friends, others as enemies. Bees are important because they pollinate crops and wild plants. They also give us honey and several other products. We fear bees and wasps for their stings, which can kill if the victim has a strong allergic reaction. However, bee venom contains chemicals that are used in medicine. Wasps help us by killing huge numbers of pests that feed on farmers' crops.

Plant-eating ants damage gardens and orchards, and can spoil food stores. Some types of ants protect aphids, which are a pest in gardens, but other ants hunt and kill caterpillars and other crop-harming pests. In tropical countries, termites cause great damage in plantations and orchards and to wooden houses. However, even termites play an important role in the cycle of life in their natural habitats.

Did you know? Termite control is a multi-billion dollar industry.

▲ **WONDERFUL WAX**
Bees are much more helpful than harmful to people. They do not just give us honey — they also produce beeswax, which is used to make polish and candles, like the ones shown here. Some people eat royal jelly, which young bees feed on, because it is healthy and nourishing.

◄ **WASP SAVES CABBAGE**
This hornet is eating a cabbage white caterpillar, which feeds on cabbage plants and is a pest for farmers and gardeners. Hornets are among the many wasp species that help farmers and gardeners by killing large numbers of insects that harm crops and prize plants. Some people spray cabbages and other plants to keep caterpillars at bay but this kills all sorts of harmless insects too.

▲ FRUIT FARMERS' ENEMY

In warm parts of the USA, leafcutter ants can become a major pest in plantations and orchards. These insects need large quantities of leaves to feed the fungi in their fungus gardens. A large colony of leafcutters can strip a fruit tree bare of leaves in a single night.

▲ NATURAL PEST CONTROL

These weaver ants are being used to control pests in an orange orchard. In China, weaver ant nests have been sold for the last 2,000 years, making them the earliest-known form of natural pest control. Farmers hang the nests in their trees and the ants eat the harmful pests.

◄ TASTY TERMITE

This man from West Africa is eating a fat, juicy termite queen, which is considered to be a delicacy in that part of the world. Social insects, including adult termites and young wasps, bees and ants, are eaten in many parts of the world, including Australia. In Western countries, people are squeamish about eating insects, but in some developing countries, tasty and nourishing insects provide up to 10 per cent of the animal protein in people's diets.

EATING YOUR WORDS ►

Wood-eating termites have damaged this book. Termites also cause major damage to timber structures in some parts of the world. Some species burrow under buildings, where they damage the wooden foundations. People often do not even know the termites are there until the damage is done and the wood is eaten away. When they are found in time, people try to kill them by using chemical insecticides.

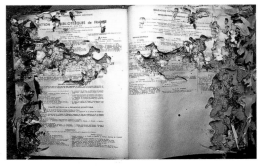

195

Insect Conservation

Just as insects affect our lives, so we affect the lives of insects. As human populations expand, we change the wild places where insects live. For example, large areas of tropical rainforest are being felled for timber or fuel, and to build settlements. This threatens the survival of the forest's plants and animals, including thousands of insect species. In developed countries all over the world, farms cover large areas that used to be wild. Crops are a feast for many insects, so their numbers multiply quickly and they become pests. Many farmers use chemical insecticides to protect their crops from the pests, but these chemicals kill 'helpful' insects along with the pests.

All over the world, conservationists fight to save rare animal species, such as tigers. It is important that we start to protect insects, too.

▲ POISON SPRAY
A tractor sprays insecticide over a field. The poisonous chemicals kill not only pests but also other insects such as bees, which pollinate flowers, and wasps, which prey on the pests. Some types of insecticide are now banned because they damage and pollute the natural world. Herbicides designed to control weeds also kill wild plants that insects feed on.

◄ FOREST DESTRUCTION
A forest is being felled for timber. The tropical rainforests contain over half of all known animal species, including thousands of insects. Destroying forests affects not only large animals but also tiny insects. Experts fear that some insects in these huge forests may become extinct before they have even been identified.

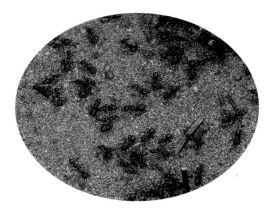

◄ PROTECTED BY LAW

In temperate forests, wood ant colonies do a vital job in preying on insects that harm the forest. In Aachen, Germany, in 1880, the wood ant became the first insect to be protected by a conservation law. It is now protected in several other European countries. Foresters also help to protect the insects by screening off their mounds to prevent people from stealing the young ants to use as fish food. Although one wood ants' nest may contain up to a million insects, including several hundred queens, it is still vulnerable to human destruction.

HELPING THE FOREST ►

Termites become our enemies when they move into our houses and eat wooden beams and furniture. People kill them using poisonous chemicals. In the wild, however, even these unpopular insects do a useful job. As they munch through leaves and wood, they help to break down plant matter so the goodness it contains returns to fertilize the soil.

◄ RARE BEE

A long-tongued bumblebee feeds from a field bean flower. This and several other crops can be pollinated only by bumblebees with long tongues. In some areas, however, domestic honeybees now thrive at the expense of the native long-tongued bees. When the long-tongued bees become scarce, the plants that depend on them for pollination are threatened too.

VITAL FOR POLLINATION ►

Many of the most popular fruits and vegetables are pollinated by honeybees. These include apples, pears, melons, onions, carrots and turnips. Honeybees also pollinate other important crops, such as cotton. Experts estimate that up to a third of all human goods depend on bees for pollination.

Butterflies in Peril

Increasing numbers of butterfly and moth
species are becoming rare or even endangered.
Their homes are lost when forests are cut down,
hedgerows are pulled up, wetlands are drained
and fields are sprayed with pesticides. All wild
creatures have been endangered to some extent
by human activity, but butterflies and moths
have suffered more than most. The life of each
species is dependent on a particular range of
food plants. Any change in the habitat that
damages food plants can threaten butterflies
and moths. For example, the ploughing up of
natural grassland has significantly reduced the
numbers of Regal Fritillary in
North America, while tourism in
mountain areas may kill off the
magnificent Apollo butterfly.

▲ **MORPHO PENDANT**
Millions of blue morpho
butterflies are collected and
made into jewellery. Only the
brightly coloured males are
collected, but this leaves the
females without mates to
fertilize their eggs.

▼ **A RARE SIGHT**
The false ringlet is probably Europe's most
endangered butterfly. The drainage
of its damp grassland
habitats has led to its
disappearance from all
but a few areas.

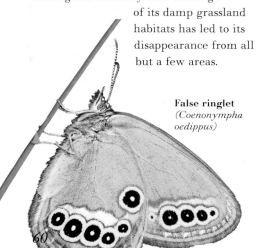

False ringlet
(*Coenonympha
oedippus*)

▲ **WANTED DEAD OR ALIVE?**
In the 1800s, millions of butterflies were caught
and killed by collectors. At the time, their
activities had little effect on populations because
so many butterflies remained in habitats that
were undisturbed. The destruction of habitat
since the 1800s has made some butterflies very
rare. Collecting even a few specimens now could
push some species towards extinction.

Did you know? *The large blue butterfly became extinct in Britain in 1979, but has been reintroduced to certain areas.*

▼ TWO-PRONGED ATTACK

The scarlet swallowtail butterfly is found only in the Philippines. It is now under threat because the rainforests it inhabits are being destroyed by urban development. Thoughtless collectors also trap this insect as a highly prized specimen.

▲ CLEARED AWAY

Rainforests are cut down and burned by developers to create new farmland and towns. Many species of butterfly and moth are threatened by the destruction of rainforest habitat.

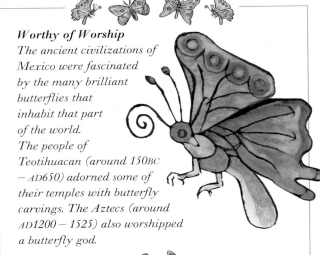

Scarlet swallowtail butterfly
(Papilio rumanzovia)

▲ NO HOME TO GO TO

The Kentish glory moth became extinct in England in the 1960s. This happened because the birch woods in which it lived were destroyed.

Worthy of Worship
The ancient civilizations of Mexico were fascinated by the many brilliant butterflies that inhabit that part of the world. The people of Teotihuacan (around 150BC – AD650) adorned some of their temples with butterfly carvings. The Aztecs (around AD1200 – 1525) also worshipped a butterfly god.

Saving Spiders

Most people are scared of spiders. With their long legs, hairy bodies and a habit of lurking in dark corners, these little creatures have not made themselves popular. Yet spiders are truly fascinating animals. Only a handful are dangerous to people, and medicines, called antivenins, can now help people recover quickly from a deadly spider's bite. Many spiders are useful in helping to control insect pests in our homes as well as on crops and in gardens. In most countries it is considered bad luck to kill a spider, but people are their greatest threat. We destroy their habitats and reduce their numbers in the wild by collecting some species to be sold as pets.

▲ NO FEAR

This man is obviously unafraid of spiders. He is quite happy to have a tarantula walk over his face. One of the greatest threats to spiders is our fear of them. People kill often harmless spiders just because they are scared. Some experts think we are born with a fear of spiders. This may be because a few were dangerous to our distant ancestors.

◄ HOUSE GUEST

House spiders are far from rare. In cooler, temperate countries, they are found in most people's homes. The common house spider leaves unwelcome, dusty sheet webs, called cobwebs, in the corners of rooms and against windows. A maze of trip wires across the surface of the web traps earwigs, flies and other household pests. House spiders may live for several years, quietly clearing our homes of insects.

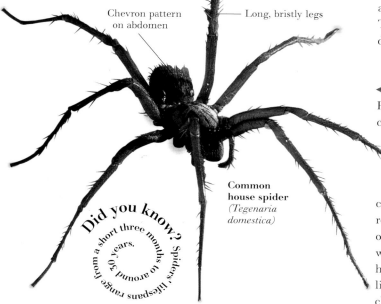

Chevron pattern on abdomen — Long, bristly legs

Common house spider
(Tegenaria domestica)

Did you know? Spiders' lifespans range from a short three months to around 30 years.

◀ HABITATS IN DANGER

People destroy and pollute the places in which spiders and many other animals live. Clearing tropical rainforests, such as this one in Paraguay, South America, is particularly destructive. A huge variety of species of spiders live in the rainforest, many of them not yet known to scientists.

◀ SPIDERS SAVING US

This Piaroa shaman (medicine man) from Venezuela, South America, uses a tarantula hunting mask as part of a ceremony. In Europe and America, spiders have been used in the past to treat malaria, the plague, toothaches and headaches. Sometimes the spiders were hung in a bag around the neck or eaten.

Little Miss Muffett

Miss Muffett was the daughter of the Reverend Thomas Muffett, a spider expert. When she was ill, her father made her eat crushed spiders as a cure. This made her terrified of spiders. A fear of spiders is called arachnophobia.

REALLY RARE ▶

Fewer than 20 species of spiders around the world are listed as threatened with extinction. They include the ladybird spider shown here. However, there must be hundreds or even thousands more spiders in danger that we do not know about yet. Spiders need our protection. For example, the Mexican red-knee tarantula is now rare in the wild because of over-collection by the pet trade. Mexican red-knee tarantulas that have been bred in captivity may help this species to survive.

Ladybird spider
(*Eresus niger*)

201

Snakes Alive

Some snakes are killed because people are afraid of them. Farmers often kill snakes to protect their farm animals and workers, although many snakes actually help farmers by eating pests. In some countries snakes are killed for food or used to make medicines. To help snakes survive, people need to take action to preserve their habitats, so that snakes can live in safety.

▲ FINDING OUT MORE
Scientists use an antenna to pick up signals from a transmitter fitted to a rattlesnake. This allows them to track the snake. The more we can learn about snakes, the easier it is to protect them.

▲ TROPHY
There are still those who shoot snakes for recreation. The hunters put the snake's rattle or head on display as a trophy demonstrating their sporting achievements.

► SNAKES IN DANGER
Snakes, such as this Dumeril's boa, are in danger of dying out. Threats include people taking them from the wild and road building in places where they live.

▼ **ROUND-UP**

This show in North America demonstrates the skill of capturing a rattlesnake. Today, rattlesnake hunts are not as common as they once were.

▲ **USING SNAKE SKINS**

Snake skins have been used for many years to make jewellery. Some species have declined as a result of intensive killing for skins in some areas. Recently, countries such as Sri Lanka and India have banned the export of snake skins.

Did you know? Legend says St Patrick banished snakes from Ireland to rid the country of evil.

▼ **PET SNAKES**

Some people like to keep pet snakes. However, they can do very little and are not happy in captivity. Snakes can lose the ability to hunt and dislike being kept in a confined space.

Crocodile Conflict

Many people only ever see a crocodile or an alligator in a story book, on the television or at the cinema. These reptiles are often portrayed as huge, fierce monsters that attack and eat humans. Such images have given crocodiles and their relatives a bad name. A few large crocodiles, such as the Nile and saltwater crocodiles, can be very dangerous. But most are timid creatures that are no threat to humans. Humans are a much bigger threat to crocodiles than they are to us. People hunt them for their skins to make handbags, shoes and belts. Traditional Oriental medicines are made from many of their body parts and their bones are ground up to add to fertilizers and animal feed. Crocodile meat and eggs are cooked and eaten, while perfume is made from their sex organs, musk and urine.

▲ LURKING DANGER
The barely visible head of an American alligator proves why swimming is not allowed in this lake. Alligators do occasionally attack people but this usually happens only when humans have invaded their habitat or disturbed their nests or hatchlings.

► CROCODILE DUNDEE
One of the most dangerous and aggressive crocodiles is the saltwater crocodile, or 'saltie', which appeared in the film *Crocodile Dundee*. In the film, Mick 'Crocodile' Dundee, saves an American journalist from a surprise attack by a saltie. An adult saltie can grow up to 7m long and is likely to view a human entering its territory as a possible meal.

Krindlekrax

In Philip Ridley's 1991 story, Krindlekrax, *a baby crocodile from a zoo escapes into a sewer and grows enormous on a diet of discarded toast. It becomes the mysterious monster Krindlekrax, which lurks beneath the pavements of Lizard Street. Krindlekrax is eventually tamed by the weedy hero of the book, Ruskin Splinter, who wedges a medal down the crocodile's throat. He agrees to take the medal away if Krindlekrax will go back to the sewer and never come back to Lizard Street again.*

▲ SKINS FOR SALE

These saltwater crocodile skins are being processed for tanning. Tanning converts the hard, preserved skin into soft, flexible leather that can be made into bags, wallets, shoes and other goods. Some crocodile skin products are made from animals that were caught in the wild. But many skins come from crocodiles raised in specially created farms.

▲ ALLIGATOR WALKABOUT

An American alligator walks through a camp-site, giving the campers a close-up view. Attacks out of the water are rare – the element of surprise is lost and alligators cannot move as fast on land. Meetings like this are harmless.

A false, glass eye has been inserted into the head.

▶ KILLED FOR A SOUVENIR

A baby Siamese crocodile was killed so that its head could be made into this souvenir key-ring. Few tourists ever manage to see a wild crocodile, but if they buy souvenirs such as this, it means more animals will be killed for a cruel trade.

205

Croc Conservation

Although people are frightened of crocodiles and their relatives, they are a vital part of the web of life in many parts of the world. Crocodiles dig water holes that help other animals survive in dry seasons and they clean up the environment by eating dead animals. Scientists find crocodiles interesting because they are good at fighting disease and rarely develop cancers. They are also fascinating to everyone as survivors from a prehistoric lost world. We need to find out more about wild crocodiles so that we can help them survive in the future. Some species, such as the American alligator, the saltwater crocodile and the gharial have already been helped by conservation projects. But much more work needs to be done. If we are to save wild crocodiles, we must preserve their habitats, stop illegal poaching and smuggling, and breed rare species in captivity for release into the wild.

▲ **CROCODILE FARM**
Tourists watch a wrestler show off his skill at a crocodile farm. The farm breeds crocodiles for their skins, and attracts tourists for extra income. Farms help to stop crocodiles being taken from the wild. The Samutprakan Crocodile Farm in Thailand has helped to save the rare Siamese crocodile from dying out by breeding the species in captivity.

▶ **RESEARCH REFUGE**
Research at the Rockefeller Wildlife Refuge in Louisiana, USA, helped to work out the best way of rearing American alligators in captivity. They are brought up in hothouses where temperature, humidity, diet and disease can all be controlled. The alligators are played music so they will be less disturbed by outside noises. In these conditions, alligators grow more than 1m a year – much faster than in the wild.

This tag on the foot of a black caiman helps identify it once it has been released into the wild. If the animal is caught again, it can be measured and weighed and the figures compared with previous records. This shows how well the animal is surviving in the wild.

▲ INTO THE FUTURE

This boy from Guyana is holding a baby dwarf caiman. Small numbers of caimans are sold as exotic pets. If people are paid more money for a living specimen than a dead one, they are less likely to kill crocodiles for skins. Educating people about why crocodiles are important is necessary to ensure their future.

► FEEDING TIME

A Nile crocodile is fed at a breeding station in South Africa. Crocodiles grow well on ranches or farms where they are fed properly. These places also provide information about the biology, health and feeding patterns of the reptiles.

◄ OFF TO A NEW HOME

A row of black caimans, reared on a ranch in Bolivia, wait to be flown to the Beni Biosphere Reserve, where they will be protected. The number of wild black caimans has dropped dramatically, and the animals they used to eat have increased as a result. This has caused problems for people, such as capybaras eating crops and piranhas attacking cattle.

Raptors at Risk

Birds of prey have few natural enemies. In many habitats they are the top predators. Wild birds of prey have only one thing to fear — humans. Over the centuries, people have hunted raptors as pests because they have occasionally killed livestock, such as game birds. Recently people have killed birds of prey indirectly by using pesticides on seeds and crops. When birds eat contaminated animals, pesticides build up in their own bodies and eventually poison them. Even when they do not kill, some pesticides weaken eggshells, which affects breeding success. Many birds of prey are now protected by law. This, and the use of safer farm chemicals, has led to a recovery in the numbers of several species. However, in some countries the indiscriminate shooting of migrating birds is still a threat, as is the destruction of habitats in which they live.

▲ TRIGGER HAPPY
A shooting enthusiast takes aim. A dog stands nearby, ready to retrieve the fallen bird. Raptors are shot by irresponsible hunters every year, especially as they flock together when migrating.

▲ GRIM WARNING
A dead hawk is left dangling on a piece of rope. This age-old practice is used by farmers and gamekeepers to warn other birds of prey to stay away from their livestock.

◀ RARE GIANT
The Philippine eagle is one of the largest birds of prey and also one of the rarest. This is because the tropical forest it inhabits is being destroyed to create farmland and places for people to live. The Philippine eagle gets its name from the Philippine Islands, where it lives. It eats large birds and sometimes even catches monkeys.

◄ DEADLY BUILD-UP

This sparrowhawk has been poisoned. It has preyed on smaller birds that have eaten seeds or insects sprayed with chemical pesticides. Gradually, the chemicals built up in the sparrowhawk's body until they made it ill, finally causing its death.

Did you know? Barn owls and kites are killed by eating poison-resistant rats.

Alice and the Griffin
A griffin sits next to Alice in a scene from Alice's Adventures in Wonderland. *The griffin is a mythical creature. According to legend, it had the head and wings of an eagle but the body of a lion.*

▲ HIT AND RUN

A barn owl lies dead at the roadside, battered by a passing vehicle the night before. Motor vehicles kill thousands of birds every day and every night. At night, owls often hunt for small prey, such as mice and voles, in roadside verges and hedges. Their habit of flying slowly, close to the ground puts them in danger from passing cars and trucks.

Hood

Perch

Falcons and Falconry

Hunting with birds of prey is called falconry or hawking. It has been a popular sport in the Middle East for thousands of years. Today falconry has many followers in other parts of the world. Falconers use a variety of birds of prey for hunting. In the past, many of these birds were taken from the wild, and some still are. This puts wild populations in danger. For example, the goshawk became extinct in Britain, partly because its eggs and chicks were taken by falconers. Today it is back in the wild and flourishing, after having been reintroduced. Falconers need skill and patience to train a bird. First they must gain the bird's trust so that it will sit and feed on the fist. Then the bird must be trained to get fit and to learn to chase prey. Falconers fly birds on long lines, called creances, before allowing them to fly free.

▲ KEPT IN THE DARK

This picture displays two essential features of falconry equipment, or furniture. The leather hood is used when the bird is on the perch and also when it is taken out hunting. Falcons such as the one above need a flat block perch to rest on.

► ANCIENT PURSUIT

An Arab falconer proudly displays a falcon as it perches on a strong leather glove on his fist. Falconry has been a popular sport in the Middle East ever since it began there more than 3,000 years ago. The favourite birds of Arab falconers are the saker and the peregrine falcon.

210

► **KITTED OUT**

This lanner falcon is about to fly back to its handler. A leash is threaded through a ring (swivel) on the jess, which is attached to the leg of the falcon. A bell helps the falconer to locate the bird if it flies off.

Bell

Jess

▲ **LURING AND STOOPING**

Moving at speed, a lanner falcon chases a lure being swung by a falconer. Falconers use lures to get falcons fit and agile and teach them to be persistent hunters. They swing the lure around their bodies or high in the air, tempting the bird to fly at it and stoop (dive swiftly).

Did you know? Many falconry centres breed birds to protect those in the wild.

▲ **A BIRD ON THE HAND**

The first stage in training a falcon is to get it to sit on the fist whilst tethered. When it first does this, the bird should be rewarded with a piece of meat. Soon, it should actively step up, then jump on the fist to feed.

▲ **A SPORT OF KINGS**

In one scene on the famous Bayeux tapestry, King Harold of England is seen riding with a hawk on his fist. The tapestry portrays events leading up to the Battle of Hastings and the conquest of England by the Normans in 1066. Hawking, or falconry, was a favourite sport of noblemen in the Middle Ages.

Wild Horses

While domestic breeds of horses and asses multiply, their wild cousins fight for survival. The only wild horse that is still plentiful in its natural range is Africa's plains zebra. All of the other species live in small, isolated groups, and many are in danger of extinction. Some horses are bred in zoos and then returned to the wild in protected reserves.

Feral horses and asses are also in danger. These domestic animals gone wild are often considered pests and are shot or poisoned. The feral burro (ass) in North America is blamed for the decline of native bighorn sheep. Burros damage the topsoil and compete with the sheep for food and water. Nevertheless, the burro is protected by law, and charities have been set up to help the free-ranging herds.

▲ SAVED FOR THE FUTURE
Przewalski's horse once lived in the Altai Mountains of Mongolia. It disappeared from its natural habitat in 1968. Before the species became extinct, 13 were taken into captivity and bred in zoos all over the world. Now their descendants are being returned to the wild. Sixty horses have been reintroduced in a specially created mountain steppe reserve in Mongolia.

◄ UPSETTING THE BALANCE
Like all feral herds living on islands off the east coast of North America, Cumberland Island horses may upset the delicate island ecology. Birdwatchers say the horses should be removed as they are not natural. But the National Parks Service protects the horses. There is a rich range of wildlife on these islands, including feral hogs.

◄ CONTROLLED POPULATION
Chincoteaguen feral horses are kept
at the Virginia end of Assateague
Island off the east coast of North
America. They are kept separate
from the Assateague ponies, another
feral group. The Chincoteague
Volunteer Fire Company keeps the
herd to below 150 animals. By doing
this, they hope to lessen damage to
the island ecology. Each year, some
Chincoteague ponies are sold to help
pay for the upkeep of the feral herd.

► BACK FROM THE BRINK
The onager is one of the smallest, fastest and
nimblest members of the horse family. It is a
subspecies of the Asiatic wild ass and lives in
northern Iran. Intense hunting caused a huge
population decline, and many were pushed
out by fighting in World War I. Recently,
the onager's numbers have been increasing.

▲ PROTECTED MUSTANGS
Life is not always easy for feral mustangs.
They must survive harsh winters in the
mountains. In many states, people keep
a watchful eye on them, and herds are
protected by government organizations.

▲ BORN FREE
A feral foal has the chance of a more natural life
than its domesticated cousins. But horses are one of
the animals that have thrived because of humans.
There are about 60 million domestic horses in the
world, far more than could be supported naturally.

213

Brought Back to Life

▲ HORSE OR ZEBRA?

The quagga looked like a cross between a zebra and a horse. It had stripes on its forequarters, like a zebra, but its hindquarters were plain, like those of a horse.

In the past few centuries, numerous creatures have become extinct because of over-hunting, or the destruction of their habitat. But it is now possible to recreate extinct species for release back into the wild. Scientists in South Africa are breeding an extinct zebra subspecies called the quagga, which died out over 100 years ago. Analysis of DNA from the cells of a quagga skin in a museum showed that the animal was a subspecies of the plains zebra. Suitable plains zebras with paler stripes were selected to start a breeding programme to bring the quagga back to life.

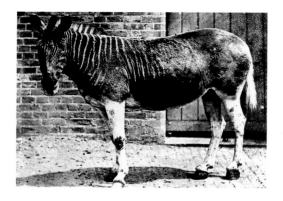

▲ SWIFT DECLINE

The quagga lived in a barren area of South Africa. Early settlers thought that it competed with their sheep and goats for the sparse grass. Millions of quaggas were slaughtered, many simply for sport. Some were transported to zoos. Breeding quaggas was not thought necessary because everyone believed there were plenty in the wild. The last quagga died in Amsterdam Zoo on 12 August 1883.

▲ NEW BEGINNING

Nine plains zebras like this one were chosen for the Quagga Project. In 1998, descendants of these nine were released in Karoo National Park. They are the only zebras there so will only breed among themselves. The offspring that are most quagga-like in each generation are selected for the next stage of breeding. It is a long process because it takes two to three years for a zebra to become sexually mature.

◄ GETTING CLOSER
One of the zebras from the Quagga Project shows that it is losing its zebra stripes. A descendant of the nine original plains zebras, it is browner and more quagga-like. It is hoped that eventually a foal will be born that matches the appearance of the extinct animal exactly.

▲ SURVIVOR OF THE STEPPES

The konik pony (above) comes from Poland. It is a descendant of the tarpan, a primitive pony that survived in the wild until the 1800s. The tarpan lived on the steppes of eastern Europe and western Asia. Its genetic make-up was identified by taking DNA from the konik and others of its descendants. Scientists selected the most tarpan-like animals and set up a breeding programme like the one for bringing back the quagga.

▲ RETURNED TO THE WILD
The Polish government are trying to recreate the tarpan. They released Przewalski's stallions (above) and tarpan-like mares, such as koniks and Icelandic horses, into two Polish nature reserves. Today, horses almost identical to the tarpan run wild there. Tarpans were victims of their own success. The stallions were fierce fighters and could take over harems of different breeds. This diluted the tarpan breed.

Elephants in Peril

Today wild elephants are in great danger. Experts warn that these animals must be protected if they are to survive in the future. Asian elephants are most at risk, with only between 36,000 and 44,000 individuals left in the wild. The main cause of their decline is humans taking their land. Activities such as building houses, mining, growing crops and constructing dams take up a lot of space. In Africa, the biggest threat to elephants is the ivory trade. African elephants have bigger tusks than Asian elephants and are therefore more valuable to hunters. Although the ivory trade was banned in 1989, it will take a long time for elephant numbers to recover.

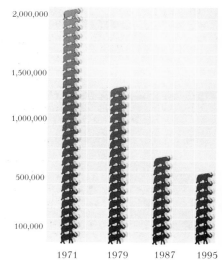

POPULATION CRASH ▲
Between 1971 and 1989, the number of elephants in Africa more than halved, from 2 million to 609,000. Up to 300 elephants were killed each day. More than 90% were killed illegally by poachers.

Did you know? Elephant meat is sold as food in some Asian countries.

◄ IVORY BONFIRE
In 1989, the Kenyan government burned US $3.6 million worth of ivory on this huge bonfire. They did this in order to support the worldwide ban on the trade in ivory. However, poachers will go on killing elephants illegally as long as people are prepared to pay huge sums of money for the tusks.

◀ WHITE GOLD

People have carved ivory for tens of thousands of years. Carvings in mammoth ivory have been found that are more than 27,000 years old. In ancient Egypt, both hippo and elephant ivory were carved. Ivory makes an ideal material for trade because even a small amount has a very high value. It is easy to carve but hard enough to last, and has a smooth, cool surface.

▲ KILLED BY POACHERS

When poachers kill elephants, they only want the tusks. They leave the rest of the elephant to rot. Before the ban on ivory trading was set up, an African poacher could earn hundreds of dollars for just one pair of tusks. It would take the poacher a year to earn this much money in an ordinary job.

▼ ELEPHANTS OR PEOPLE?

These elephants are invading a farmer's home and fields in Kenya, east Africa. The human population of Kenya is expected to double by the year 2020, putting enormous pressure on the land. Finding enough land for both people and elephants will be a problem. Elephants will not be able to roam freely, as they have been able to do in the past. Instead, they will be confined to special areas.

▲ TOO MANY ELEPHANTS

African elephant feet are sometimes sold to raise money for conservation. These animals were killed legally in a National Park where elephant numbers had grown too high.

Protecting Elephants

Elephants need to be conserved if they are to survive. Many African and Asian countries have set aside areas of land called national parks or nature reserves. Here, elephants are protected from the threat of poachers. However, this is not a perfect solution. Elephants in reserves are so well protected that their numbers steadily rise. Confined to a protected area, they eventually eat everything within it. Rangers are then forced to kill some elephants to let others live. Other elephant conservation efforts include banning the trade in ivory. Several alternatives to ivory exist which are not a threat to wildlife, including plastics, resins and the nuts of a South American palm tree.

▲ **WELL LOOKED AFTER**
A zoo elephant has its foot cleaned with a hoof knife. Zoos play a major role in conserving animals. But elephants are not often bred in zoos because bulls are difficult to handle and can be dangerous.

▲ **WALRUS WORRIES**
When the trade in elephant ivory was banned in 1989, poachers turned their attention to walrus ivory instead. During 1989, poachers in speedboats shot at least 12,000 Alaskan walruses, whose tusks can grow almost a metre long.

▲ **POACHING PATROLS**
Guards in a national park in southern Africa hold wire traps left by poachers. Protecting elephants from poachers is dangerous work. As well as removing traps left for elephants, guards may become involved in gun battles with poachers trying to kill elephants.

◀ ELEPHANT TRAVELS

Sometimes, elephants are moved to areas where they have better chances of survival. Moving elephants is not an easy thing to do. Getting these huge, heavy animals into a truck or an aeroplane can be a tricky business. Sometimes a whole elephant family is moved. This helps these sensitive animals get over the trauma of being captured and taken somewhere new. They then settle into their new home more easily.

◀ SUPPORT GROUPS

Conservation groups such as Elefriends in the UK raise money to help conservation work in the wild. They also persuade people not to buy and trade in ivory.

▲ BRINGING UP BABY

With a great deal of patience, care and understanding, orphaned baby elephants, such as this African elephant, can be raised in National Parks and returned to the wild. Raising a baby elephant is just as hard work as raising a baby human.

▶ BIG ATTRACTION

Tourists pay to watch elephants in national parks. This money is used to help run the parks and look after the elephants. It is also used to improve the lives of people living nearby. Many of these people have given up their land to save the elephants.

Bears in Danger

Of the eight species of bears living today, six are considered to be endangered. Only polar bears and American black bears are holding their own, and even they would not survive without considerable protection. Bears face many dangers. Their habitat is shrinking as natural areas are used to provide homes and farmland for people. Cubs are kept as pets but sold when they grow into troublesome adults. Many wild bears do not reach old age because they are shot by hunters. Hides and heads are used as wall hangings and trophies. In many parts of the world bear meat is eaten. Blood, bones and body parts are used in traditional Oriental medicines and as good luck charms. By far the biggest threat to bears is from poaching to supply the medicine trade.

▲ **DANCING BEAR**
A sloth bear is made to dance in India. Despite laws against it, bear cubs are taken from the wild. They are then taught to dance using cruel methods and kept in poor conditions.

◄ **CIRCUS ACT**
Bears have long been popular circus animals. Their ability to walk on their hind feet makes them appear almost human. These agile and clever animals are forced to perform tricks such as skipping, riding a bicycle and walking the tightrope. Performing bears are often badly cared for and may be made to work all year round.

▲ MAN VERSUS BEAST

Bears have been entertaining people for centuries. This carving from the AD300s depicts gladiators fighting bears in the arena. Both brown bears and polar bears were killed to entertain the audience.

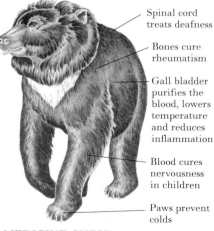

Spinal cord treats deafness

Bones cure rheumatism

Gall bladder purifies the blood, lowers temperature and reduces inflammation

Blood cures nervousness in children

Paws prevent colds

▲ MEDICINE CHEST

Bear organs are important in Oriental medicine. The most valuable part is the gall bladder, said to cure a whole host of ailments including fevers. Many bears are killed for their gall bladder alone.

◄ GOOD FOOD

We can learn a lot from bears. Native Americans discovered that many plants eaten by bears have medicinal properties. The Cheyenne treat diarrhoea with a plant called bear's foot and the Crow use bear root to cure sore throats.

► MEASURING UP

A scientist takes measurements from a tranquillized bear. A better understanding of the biology and behaviour of bears will hopefully secure them a safer future.

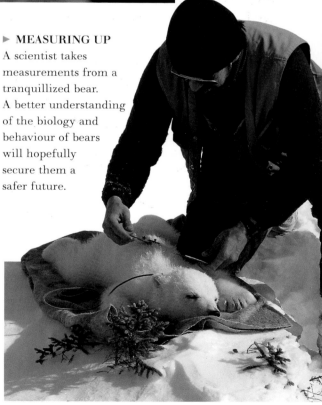

Churchill's

Each autumn, polar bears come into close contact with people at the isolated Canadian town of Churchill on the shores of Hudson Bay. The bears are on their way from the inland forests where they spend the summer, to the ice of the bay where they hunt. Often they arrive before the ice forms and cause a lot of trouble while they hang around with nothing to do. Some bears head for town and scare the local townsfolk. Others make for the town dump. The bears are chased away but some come back. Frequent offenders are tranquillized and taken somewhere safe. Despite the problems they cause, the bears have become a tourist attraction. People come from all over the world to see so many polar bears gathered together.

LOOKING FOR TROUBLE
This bear has picked up the tantalizing scent of tourists. Many visitors arrive to see the bears each year. They travel about in special buses called tundra buggies, where they are safe from the powerful and inquisitive bears.

READY FOR REMOVAL
A researcher cautiously tests a tranquillized polar bear to make sure it is fully sedated. He holds a gun in case the polar bear is not as sleepy as it seems to be and attacks. Polar bears at Churchill occasionally threaten people. They are tranquillized and moved a safe distance away or locked up in a trap until the ice refreezes.

Ice Bears

BEAR BACK

A polar bear keeps cool by rolling in a patch of snow while it waits for the ice to form on Hudson Bay. The days can be warm in the Arctic autumn. Polar bears have thick fur and may overheat if they are not able to cool down.

FAST FOOD

A bear scavenges through the town rubbish dump. This is a favourite rendezvous spot. Household rubbish provides easy food for hungry bears unable to hunt.

FREE FLIGHT

A sedated bear is carried away in a net strung under a helicopter. This is a quick way to move a large animal, but it is also very expensive.

THE SIN BIN

A rogue bear is released from a bear trap. Unfortunately, bears have a well-developed homing instinct and often appear in town again. Persistent offenders are kept in a polar bear jail until the ice refreezes.

DANGER
BEAR TRAP

Big Cat Casualties

The earliest record of people using big cat pelts (skins) dates from 6500BC. It comes from the archaeological site of Çatal Hüyük, in Turkey, where there is evidence that dancers wore leopard skins. Much more recently, in the 19th and 20th centuries, many wealthy people hunted big cats for the thrill of the chase. The skins of the animals killed were used to decorate the hunters' houses, and their heads were hung as trophies on the walls. Today, this kind of hunting is rare, and every effort is made to prevent it.

▲ LION HUNT
Egyptian rulers hunted lions from horse-drawn chariots. Hieroglyphics (picture writing) tell us of Pharaoh Amenophis III (1405–1367BC) who killed over 100 lions in the ten years of his rule. Some experts now think that the Egyptians may have bred lions specially to hunt them.

TIGER-HUNTING PRINCE ▶
This old painting on cotton shows an Indian prince hunting a tiger from the back of his elephant. Tiger hunting was a very popular pastime for many centuries in India. It was declared illegal in the 1970s.

▼ GREAT WHITE HUNTER

A hunting party proudly displays its tiger trophy. This photograph was taken in the 1860s. When India was under British rule, tiger hunting was considered to be a great sport by the British. Uncontrolled, ruthless hunting was a major cause of the tiger's dramatic fall in numbers.

▲ RITUAL ROBES

The Zulu chief Mangosothu Buthelezi wears wild cat skins on special occasions, like many African leaders and tribal healers. They are a sign of his rank and high status.

Did you know? The rarest of all the big cats is the snow leopard from the Himalayas.

◄ SLICED UP

A leopard is skinned, having been shot in the Okavango Delta in Botswana. Some game reserves raise money for conservation by charging huge sums to hunt. This only happens when numbers of a certain species are too large for the reserve.

SECOND SKIN ►

Some people continue to think it looks good to wear a coat made from the pelts of a wild cat. Many more, however, think that the fur looks much better on the cat. Designers now use fake fur and skins dyed to look like pelts, instead.

Conserving Cats

All big cats are in danger of extinction. They are hunted not only for their skins, but also for their teeth, bones and other body parts, which are used as traditional medicines in many countries. The Convention for International Trade in Endangered Species (CITES) lists all big cats under Appendix 1, which strictly controls their import and export. For cats particularly at risk, such as the tiger, all trade is banned. There are now many protected areas throughout the world where big cats can live without human interference. These areas are often not big enough, however, so the cats leave in search of food. They then attack livestock and sometimes local farmers.

▲ **IN ANCIENT TIMES**
This Roman mosaic shows a horseman hunting a leopard. Two thousand years ago, big cats were much more widespread. Until the 20th century, cheetahs lived throughout Africa, central India and the Middle East. Hunting big cats was not a problem when there were many of them but now the situation is desperate.

▲ **INDIAN PRIDE**
The last remaining Asian lions live in the Gir National Park in north-western India. There are fewer than 300 lions living in the forest park. The Asian lion is slightly different from the African lion. It has a smaller mane and a fold of skin running between its front and back legs.

▲ **SERENGETI LION PROJECT**
This lion has been drugged so that it can be fitted with a radio collar, before being checked and then released. In the Serengeti National Park in Tanzania, scientists use methods like this to study lion behaviour.

▲ EYES ON THE BACKS OF THEIR HEADS

Villagers in the Sundarbans mangrove forests in India wear masks on the backs of their heads. Tigers attack from behind, but will not usually strike if they see a face. The largest remaining tiger population in India is in the Sundarbans. Here 50 to 60 people die each year from tiger attacks. There is obviously not enough food for the tigers, so conservationists are trying to improve the situation. Another deterrent is to set up dummies that look and smell like humans, but give out an electric shock if attacked. There are also electrified fences in some areas, and pigs are bred and released as tiger food.

▼ RADIO TRACKING

Biologists attach a radio collar to a tigress in Nepal's Chitwan National Park. To save big cats we need to understand their habits and needs. For this reason, many scientists and conservationists are studying them. It is a very difficult task since cats are secretive and often nocturnal animals. One way of gathering information is to put a radio collar on a big cat and then follow its movements. By doing this, the animal can be tracked at long range.

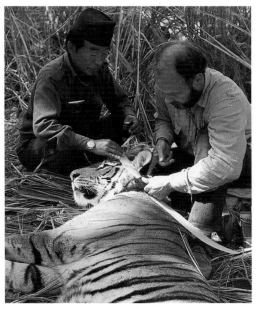

The Biggest Big Cat of All

In Egypt, an enormous statue with a human head and the body of a lion guards the Great Pyramids at Giza. This statue is the Great Sphinx. A story written in 1419BC on the Sphinx tells of a prince called Thutmose IV who fell asleep between the paws of the statue. He dreamt that the Sun god told him to take away the sand covering part of the Sphinx and he would become a king. When he awoke, Thutmose did as he had been instructed, and the dream came true.

Wolves and People

Wherever wolves and wild dogs come into contact with people, the animals are regarded as dangerous pests that will kill livestock given the chance. They are poisoned, trapped and shot, not only for their skins, but for sport. Wolves were once the most widespread carnivores in the northern hemisphere. Now they have a much reduced range, often surviving only in small, scattered groups. Several wild dog species are endangered, including the Simien wolf, the red wolf and the African hunting dog. Much of the land where these animals once lived is now being farmed. Dholes have also become very rare as their forest habitat is destroyed. Some species, such as the Falkland Island wolf, a large fox, are already extinct.

NORTH AMERICA

SOUTH AMERICA

grey wolf territories

▲ WOLF HUNT
In the Middle Ages domestic dogs were often used to kill wolves, as this Dutch engraving of 1880 shows. The last wolves were wiped out in England by 1500 and in Ireland by 1800.

Tame Wolf
This book is a first edition of the popular novel White Fang *by the American writer Jack London. Set in northern Canada, it describes how a wolf, named White Fang, is tamed and becomes a pet. In general it is not against the law to keep a wolf as a pet, but countries with restrictions require owners to have a special permit. The Call of the Wild by the same author describes how a pet dog joins a wolf pack and becomes wild.*

WHITE FANG

JACK LONDON

▲ WOLF TERRITORY

Grey wolves once had the greatest range of any wild land mammal. In the past, wolves were once common all across North America, throughout Europe, the Middle East and most of Asia. Their present range shows they have been exterminated in most of Mexico and the United States, in almost all of western Europe and over much of Asia.

▼ A CRUEL LUXURY

Fox fur was very fashionable in the early 20th century, mainly for coats. The fox fur stole (scarf) shown here uses the pelt (fur and skin) of an entire animal. In the past, furs were worn mainly to keep warm in winter. Today, however, man-made fabrics are as warm as fur, making it unnecessary and cruel to kill these animals for their pelts.

◀ NOWHERE TO RUN

A hunter in Colorado, shoulders a coyote he has shot. In country areas, farmers shoot or poison coyotes because they kill sheep and other livestock, and spread disease. Elsewhere, when coyotes and other wild dogs enter towns to scrounge scraps, they risk being shot as pests.

▲ UNDER THREAT

A Simien wolf howls high in the Ethiopian mountains. As the human population grows, more land is farmed and the animal's range is restricted. Simien wolves are shot for fur and killed by farmers as pests. There may be only 500 Simien wolves left in the wild.

Caring for Wolves

In many parts of the world, efforts are being made to save threatened wolves and wild dogs. Grey wolves have recently been reintroduced into areas where they had died out. Conservationists working to protect wolves face opposition from local farmers who fear that wolves will kill their livestock. In some reserves, wolves and wild dogs have begun to be promoted as tourist attractions. This helps people to learn about these animals and the entrance fees help to finance conservation work. Today, wolves and their relatives are gradually losing their bad image. More and more people are appreciating their admirable qualities – intelligence, loyalty and strong family ties. In the wild, these predators actually improve stocks of prey animals. By hunting mostly weak or sickly individuals, they help to ensure the survival of the fittest.

▲ **SUCCESS STORY**
Conservationists release a red wolf that was bred in captivity into a reserve in North Carolina, USA. Red wolves were once found throughout the southeastern United States. They nearly became extinct, but breeding programs have saved the species.

◄ **RADIO TRACKING**
This red wolf has been fitted with a radio collar. The collar allows scientists to track the animal as it roams the wilds. Radio tracking helps to provide scientists with valuable information about the red wolf's habits and range. Increasing such knowledge also helps conservationists with their work.

▲ STARS OF THE SHOW

Tourists on safari photograph African hunting dogs in a reserve. In recent years, such tourist attractions have earned much-needed cash for remote villages. The money helps to persuade local people not to hunt the dogs, but to see them as a valuable asset instead.

▲ KEEPING THE BALANCE

A pack of wolves feeds on a deer carcass. By targeting old and sick animals, the wolves actually help the rest of the herd to survive. They may be removing a deer whose sickness could infect others in the herd, or an old animal whose share of food could be better used to rear healthy young.

▼ SOUND OF THE WILD

For many people, the wolf is a symbol of the wilderness. In certain countries, wolves are now becoming a tourist attraction. At some centres, members of the public can even walk alongside tame wolves, petting them if they wish, accompanied, of course, by expert handlers.

▲ WOLF RESEARCH

Scientists check the teeth of a tranquillized Arctic wolf. Researchers sometimes capture the same wolves several times over the course of a number of years to study their life histories. This work helps to provide evidence of the strong family ties and keen intelligence of the wolf.

Monkeys and Us

Humans have often woven magical stories around monkey characters and some even worship monkey gods. However, people have also captured monkeys and used them cruelly.

By international law, it is illegal to buy and sell monkeys without a licence. This may be given, say, for the purposes of scientific experiments. Unfortunately, some monkeys are illegally exported, often travelling long distances in cramped and cruel conditions.

Many monkey and ape species are eaten in Africa and South-east Asia. Most are eaten by local people, for whom monkeys are a cheap source of 'bush meat'. However, more and more monkey meat is being smuggled around the world, especially into Europe and China, where it is sold illegally for very high prices. Conservationists believe that, if the bush meat trade is not stopped, many monkeys and apes could be wiped out within a few years.

▲ AT YOUR SERVICE
In Malaysia, macaques are trained to climb palm trees to pick coconuts. The agile monkeys easily scramble up to the tops of the trees, where the coconuts grow. The macaques have learned to throw the coconuts down to their human owner. Although the monkeys are captive, this task is similar to the behaviour of wild macaques.

◀ UNNATURAL PERFORMANCE
In parts of Asia, monkeys, such as this rhesus macaque, are trained to perform tricks to earn money for their human owners. Wild animals in captivity are often treated cruelly by being forced to perform in a way that is completely unnatural to them. Monkeys are not domesticated animals that have been bred to live with humans.

▲ OBEYING ORDERS

This monkey has been put in a cage to stop it escaping. The monkey will behave toward its human owner as a low-ranking male would do to a troop leader in the wild: it will cower to avoid confrontation and will try to do what the owner wants in return for access to food.

▲ FOR THE SAKE OF HUMANKIND

Live monkeys are sometimes used in scientific experiments. This is called vivisection. Some of these monkeys are injured or killed. Many scientists believe that vivisection provides important information that could reduce the suffering of human beings, but others disagree.

◀ LIFT OFF!

A space shuttle blasts off. In the early days of space travel, many monkeys were used in experiments to study weightlessness.

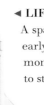

GUIDE MONKEYS ▶

Capuchins – the cleverest New World monkeys – have been taught to help disabled people. The monkeys can pick up objects such as telephones and take them to their owners, as well as perform tasks such as operating switches. Although their owners might benefit, not everyone thinks that it is right to use monkeys in this way.

Protecting Primates

When the last member of a species dies, that species is extinct. It is lost forever. In the last few decades, many people have worked to stop the rarest primate species becoming extinct. Some have started sanctuaries and zoos where animals are helped to breed away from predators. Nearly half of the world's total population of aye-ayes (one of the most threatened of Madagascar's lemurs) is in zoos because there is not enough of their natural habitat left to support them.

To save an endangered species, the cause of the threat must be addressed. This might be the destruction of the animal's habitat or the poverty of the people who hunt them. We can all affect the survival of species by making sure that we do not buy products that cause damage to their wild habitat.

Did you know? Thanks to conservationists, only one primate has become extinct in 100 years.

▲ LIFE IN A COLD CLIMATE

Woolly monkeys come from the steamy jungles of Brazil. This one lives in English woodland. The monkeys' natural habitat in Brazil is being destroyed by humans and the species is disappearing fast. At its cliff-top home in the south-west of England, this monkey is given special foods to make sure that it gets the same minerals in its diet as it would in the wild.

◀ BACK TO THE WILD

Gerald Durrell, a British conservationist, holds a red-ruffed lemur. Durrell set up a pioneering zoo on the island of Jersey. Many rare primates have been bred there, and the zoo has successfully reintroduced lemurs and tamarins to their natural habitats. The Jersey zoo teaches keepers from other zoos how to raise captive-born animals so they can be released back into the wild.

◄ HOME FROM HOME

This realistic rainforest has been created in New York's Bronx Zoo. The temperature, humidity and light are as close as possible to natural rainforest conditions. Captive primates raised in a habitat similar to their wild environment are less likely to become distressed. They will stand a better chance of survival if they are later released into the wild.

KEEPING TRACK ►

These two golden lion tamarins, born in a zoo, were released into a protected area of Brazilian forest. Scientists fitted them with radio transmitters to keep track of them. This species has been saved from extinction by being bred in zoos around the world.

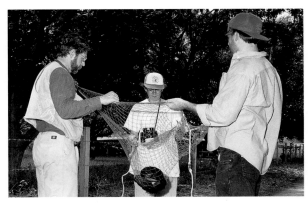

▲ IN THE BAG

Scientists have shot this howler monkey with a drugged dart. They will take some measurements, then give the monkey another drug to bring it back to consciousness. Their aim is to gain as much information as possible about the howler monkey's population structure, its diet and the diseases it suffers. This will help them to understand how to conserve the species better.

▲ SAFE SANCTUARY

This monkey, whose parents were killed by hunters, has been rescued and taken to an orphanage. Sometimes, young monkeys that were captured illegally are rescued and sent to zoos. They can't be set free, as they don't know how to survive in the wild.

Apes in Danger

Wild apes live in steadily shrinking habitats. Their woodland and forest homes have been gradually replaced by farms, grazing lands and villages. Vast areas of rainforest have been flooded by the water held back by dams, and other areas have been dug up by mining companies looking for precious metals and other minerals. Even in some protected areas, apes are still illegally hunted for their meat, or captured to be sold as pets or for medical research. In times of war, apes are further threatened by weapons such as land mines and the movement of large numbers of refugees into their habitat. People can also pass on diseases to apes, without even realizing that they have done so.

▲ A POACHER'S TOOLS
This is some of the equipment used by poachers to kill apes illegally in protected areas such as national parks. Wire snares concealed in the undergrowth can prove deadly to apes trapped in their tight grip. Traditional hunting weapons such as spears and arrows may also be used.

Did you know? There are just 630 mountain gorillas in the world.

GORILLA SKULLS ▶
Ape body parts are sometimes sold as grisly souvenirs. These gorilla skulls are for sale on a traditional African medicine stall where they are used as fetishes (a type of good luck charm). There would be no reason for poachers to kill apes if people were not prepared to buy their body parts. Gorillas are also killed for meat. Some of it feeds workers cutting down the forests. The rest is sold in city markets.

▲ FOREST DESTRUCTION

The greatest danger to apes is the destruction of their habitat, especially the rainforests. An area of rainforest the size of over 100 football pitches disappears every minute. Rainforests are cut down for their valuable timber, or burned to make way for cattle ranches or plantations of cash crops.

▲ THREAT OF WAR

In the 1990s, war in Rwanda led people to raid the mountain gorillas' national park for food and firewood. Land mines were also left in the park.

▲ DEADLY DISEASE

Apes are so similar to us that they suffer from many of the same diseases. For example, like us, apes can catch malaria, carried by mosquitoes.

FOREST FIRES ▶

In the late 1990s, forest fires raged across Borneo and Sumatra, killing many orang-utans, destroying their habitat and causing breathing problems for the survivors.

Ape Conservation

Gorillas, orang-utans, chimpanzees and bonobos are now officially recognized as endangered species. Laws have been passed to stop live apes and parts of their bodies from being bought or sold. However, laws can never give total protection to wild animals, especially when people can make large amounts of money by breaking the law. To help apes survive in the future, their habitat needs to be protected in national parks or reserves. Apes bred in captivity might one day be released into the wild, but only if suitable natural habitats can be found. Conserving apes takes much time and costs much money. Many of the countries where wild apes live have very little money and need help for conservation from richer nations. Apes are more like humans than any other animal. It will be tragic if we cannot find a way to share our future with them.

▲ GORILLAS IN THE MIST
Dian Fossey wrote about her work with mountain gorillas in *Gorillas in the Mist*, later made into a film starring Sigourney Weaver (above). The film raised awareness of the gorilla's plight.

▼ HABITAT ZOOS
Some good zoos now keep apes in large, tree-filled enclosures, which are as much like their natural habitat as possible. Breeding apes in zoos helps to increase their numbers.

western lowland gorillas
(Gorilla gorilla gorilla)

▲ TOURIST DOLLARS

Many people pay a lot of money to get close to a wild great ape, but this is too close as the ape could catch human flu. If tourists are carefully controlled, they can help ape conservation.

▼ POACHING PATROL

These wardens are patrolling the national park where mountain gorillas live. They are keeping a sharp lookout for armed poachers and their snares. If there is a shoot-out, both the wardens and the poachers could be killed.

◄ CHIMFUNSHI ORPHANAGE

David and Sheila Siddle have converted their farm in Zambia into the Chimfunshi Wildlife Orphanage to look after rescued chimps from the Congo. The Siddles have walled and fenced off their land and allow the chimps to climb trees, build nests and live like wild chimpanzees.

► LIVING ON THE EDGE

In developing countries where most families grow their own food, there is an increasing need for more land. Forests are cleared right up to the park boundary, as can be seen in this photograph, which shows the edge of the Virunga National Park in the Congo. If gorillas and elephants wander out searching for food, they are labelled 'crop raiders' by local farmers, who are desperate to protect their only source of food or income.

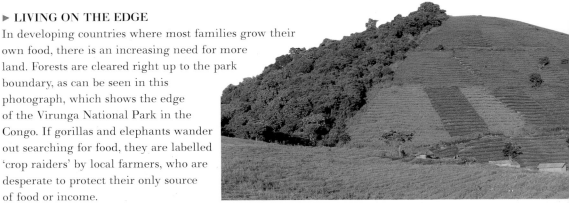

Whale Slaughter

The baleen whales and sperm whale are so big that they have no natural predators. Until a few hundred years ago, the oceans teemed with them. In the 15th and 16th centuries, whaling grew into a huge industry. Whales were killed for blubber, which could be rendered down into oils for candles and lamps. The industry expanded following the invention of an explosive harpoon gun in the 1860s, and by the 1930s nearly 50,000 whales a year were caught in the Antarctic. In 1988, commercial whaling was banned.

▲ WHALE SOAP

The sperm whale was once a prime target for whalers. They were after the waxy spermaceti from the organ in the whale's forehead. This was used to make soap.

▶ DEADLY STRUGGLE

Whalers row out from a big ship to harpoon a whale in the early 1800s. It was a dangerous occupation in those days because the dying whales could easily smash the small boats to pieces.

Did you know? Whale blubber was made into lipstick and other sorts of make-up.

▼ FIN WHALING

A modern whaler finishes cutting up a fin whale. A few whales are still caught legally for scientific purposes, but their meat ends up on the table in some countries. The fin whale used to be a favourite target for whalers because of its huge size.

◄ **PILOT MASSACRE**
Every year in the Faroe Islands of the North Atlantic, pods of pilot whales are killed, a traditional practice that has not been stopped. The blood of the dying whales turns the sea red.

Did you know? Early whalers killed their prey by throwing harpoons from rowing boats.

► **KILLER NET**
This striped dolphin died when it was caught in a drift net. It became entangled and was unable to rise to the surface to breathe. Tens of thousands of dolphins drown each year because of nets cast into the oceans.

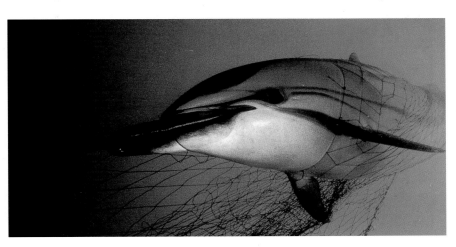

Did you know? In the 1800s baleen was used to make umbrellas.

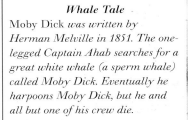

Whale Tale
Moby Dick *was written by Herman Melville in 1851. The one-legged Captain Ahab searches for a great white whale (a sperm whale) called Moby Dick. Eventually he harpoons Moby Dick, but he and all but one of his crew die.*

THE SPERMACETI WHALE

Saving the Whales

If full-scale whaling had continued, many of the great whales would now be extinct. Even today, only a few thousand blue whales, right whales and bowhead whales remain. Because they are slow breeders, it will take a long time for numbers to recover. However the grey whale and the humpback whale appear to be recovering well. These two whales are favourites among whale-watchers because they are so approachable. Whale-watching has made people aware of how remarkable whales are and why they must be protected. Dolphins and killer whales are popular at aquariums, but it is not to their benefit to keep them in captivity.

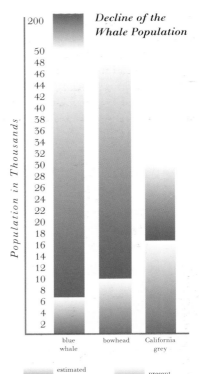

Decline of the Whale Population

Population in Thousands

200
50
48
46
44
42
40
38
36
34
32
30
28
26
24
22
20
18
16
14
12
10
8
6
4
2

blue whale   bowhead   California grey

estimated original population

present population

Did you know? *The first whale sanctuary was set up in 1945.*

▲ **GREY GREETING**
A grey whale rises to the surface near a tourist boat off the Pacific coast of Mexico. It is winter, and the grey whales have migrated to these breeding grounds from the far north. Because these animals stay close to the shore, they are easy to reach by boat.

▲ **WHALE RECOVERY**
By the middle of the 20th century, the blue, bowhead and grey whales were close to extinction. Then whaling was banned. Now populations are recovering.

▼ **HUMPBACK SPECTACULAR**
A humpback whale breaches. It hurls its 30-tonne bulk into the air, belly up, and will soon crash back to the surface. Out of all the behaviour whale-watchers come to see, this is by far the most spectacular.

► FRIENDLY FLIPPER

One bottlenose dolphin character, called Flipper (played by several dolphins) starred in a series of TV programmes and films. These focused attention on how intelligent dolphins are, yet how vulnerable they are, too.

Did you know? You can adopt your own whale by contacting your own local whale and dolphin society.

◄ WHALE-WATCHING

A boatload of whale-watchers sees the tail flukes of a humpback whale disappear as the animal starts to dive. The boat is cruising off the New England coast of the United States where some populations of humpbacks feed during the summer months.

► PERFORMING KILLER

A killer whale leaps high out of the water at an aquarium, drawing applause from the huge crowd watching. In the wild, the killer whale is a deadly predator, but in captivity — with all meals provided — it is docile and friendly. However, the benefits of keeping these creatures in captivity are not certain.

Did you know? Some countries continue to hunt whales.

Shark Encounters

Sharks are feared because they attack people. However, only a few such attacks take place each year. People are more likely to be killed on the way to the beach than be killed by a shark in the water. Fortunately, attitudes are changing. Today, people have a healthy respect for sharks, rather than a fear of them. As we come to understand sharks, instead of killing them, people want to learn more about them. Diving with sharks, even known man-eaters such as the great white shark or bull shark, is more accepted. People study sharks either from the safety of a cage or, increasingly, in the open sea without any protection. Such is our fascination with sharks that aquariums for sharks are being built all over the world. Here, more people will be able to learn about sharks at first hand, and not even get wet!

Jaws

The book and film Jaws *featured an enormous great white shark that terrorized a seaside town. The film drew great crowds and its story terrified people all over the world. It also harmed the reputation of sharks, encouraging people to see them as monsters, rather than the extraordinarily successful animals that they are.*

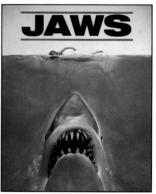

◄ FREE LUNCH

At tourist resorts in the tropics, divers can watch sharks being fed by hand. This activity is not always approved of. Sharks come to rely on this free handout, and may become aggressive if it stops. Inexperienced divers may also not know how to behave with sharks, resulting in accidents, although these are rare.

◄ ANTI-SHARK MEASURES

Anti-shark nets protect many popular South African and Australian beaches. Unfortunately, these nets not only catch sharks, like this tiger shark, but also other sea life, including dolphins and turtles. Less destructive ways of reducing people's fear of attack have yet to be invented.

► SHARK POD

Although a similar system is not yet available to bathers, one anti-shark invention seems to work for divers and, possibly, surfers, too. A shark pod can produce an electric field that interferes with the electrical sensors of a shark, encouraging the animal to keep its distance.

◄ SHARK VICTIM

Occasionally, sharks do attack people. While diving in Australian waters, Rodney Fox was attacked by a great white shark. Rodney was possibly mistaken for a seal. He is probably alive because he did not have enough blubber on him to interest the shark and he was able to get away.

MUNICIPALITY OF ROCKDALE
DANGER
SHARKS IN BOTANY BAY

▲ SHARK WARNING

On many beaches, shark warning signs are used to tell people that sharks might be present. During the day, danger of attack is low, but it increases at night, when the sharks move inshore to feed.

Sharks Attacked

Sharks take a long time to grow to adulthood. They have very few offspring and may breed only every other year. Added to these factors, the hunting and killing of sharks can quickly reduce their numbers. This happened at Achill Island, on the Irish coast, where large numbers of basking sharks quickly disappeared, after they were killed for their oil. Off the coasts of South Australia and South Africa, the great white shark was hunted as a trophy for many years. Numbers of great whites were so reduced that the hunting of them has since been banned internationally. A few countries control the fishing of sharks, to try to conserve (protect) them. However, in other countries, sharks are still hunted for shark fin soup, unusual medicines and souvenirs. They are also sold to supermarkets as shark steak. Sharks, it seems, have more to fear from people than people have to fear from sharks.

◄ WASTED SHARKS
Each summer, many sharks are killed in fishing tournaments off the east coast of the USA. Sports fishermen are now learning to tag sharks, returning them to the sea alive instead of killing them. By tagging sharks, our understanding of shark biology is increased.

▶ **CRUEL TRADE**
Caught by fishermen,
this whitetip reef shark
has had its valuable fins
removed. The shark was
then thrown back into the
sea, still alive. Without its
fins, a shark is unable to
move and, therefore, feed.
It will quickly starve to
death. This awful process,
called finning, has been
banned by some countries.

◀ **TRAVELLING INTO TROUBLE**
This tiger shark is being tagged to track its
movements. Shark tagging programmes like this
show that many sharks travelling great distances
are being netted by several fisheries along their
routes. Unless shark fishing is controlled
internationally, sharks that travel long distances
will probably disappear from the sea altogether.

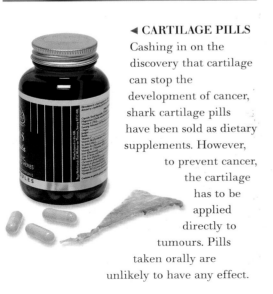

◀ **CARTILAGE PILLS**
Cashing in on the
discovery that cartilage
can stop the
development of cancer,
shark cartilage pills
have been sold as dietary
supplements. However,
to prevent cancer,
the cartilage
has to be
applied
directly to
tumours. Pills
taken orally are
unlikely to have any effect.

▲ **EXPENSIVE SOUP**
Shark fin soup is made from the dried fins
of a shark. It has been prepared by chefs in
oriental countries for over 2,000 years. The
soup was once served to show favour to an
honoured guest, and was also thought to
be a health-giving food. Today, it is sold in
cans and can be bought in supermarkets.

Glossary

abdomen
The rear section of an animal's body, which holds the reproductive organs and part of the digestive system.

adapt
To alter in some way in order to survive in changed conditions. The change usually takes place over many generations in a process called evolution.

antennae (singular antenna)
The long projections on an insect's head, which it uses to smell, touch and taste.

artery
A blood vessel that carries blood away from the heart.

arthropod
An animal without a backbone that has many jointed legs and an exoskeleton on the outside of its body. Arthropods include spiders, insects, crabs and woodlice.

binocular vision
The ability to see things with both eyes at the same time. This enables animals such as cats and wolves to judge distances accurately.

bladder
Where waste urine is stored in the body before being expelled.

breaching
When whales and dolphins leap out of the water and fall back with a great splash.

breed
An animal that belongs to one species, but has definite characteristics, such as colouring, coat markings and body shape.

camouflage
The colours or patterns on an animal's body that allow it to blend in with its surroundings.

canid
A member of the dog family. The group includes wolves, foxes and African hunting dogs.

canine
A sharp, pointed tooth that grips and pierces the skin of prey.

captivity
When animals are captured and forced to live within certain areas that they are unable to leave.

carcass
The dead body of an animal.

carnivore
An animal that feeds on the flesh of other animals.

cloaca
A chamber at the very rear of the gut in fish, amphibians, reptiles, and birds. The reproductive and urinary systems open into it.

cold-blooded
An animal whose temperature varies according to its surroundings.

colony
A group of the same species of animal or plant that live together.

conservation
Protecting living things and helping them to survive in the future.

constrictor
A snake that kills by coiling its body around its prey to suffocate it.

courtship
The process of courting or attracting an intended mating partner.

crocodilian
A member of the group of animals that includes crocodiles, alligators, gharials and caimans.

diaphragm
A sheet of muscle separating the chest cavity from the abdominal cavity of mammals. Its movement helps with breathing.

digestion
The process by which food is broken down so that it can be absorbed by the body.

domesticated
Animals that do not live in the wild but have been tamed by humans and are kept as pets, for example, cats and dogs, or farm animals, such as sheep.

dragline
The line of silk on which a spider drops down, often to escape from danger.

echo-location
The method used by toothed whales to find their prey. They send out pulses of high-pitched sounds and listen for the echoes produced when the pulses are reflected by objects in their path.

endangered
Any plant or animal that is in danger of extinction in the near future.

environment
The surroundings or conditions within which an animal lives.

equids
Horses and horse-like animals, such as asses and zebras.

evolution
The natural change of living organisms over very long periods of time, so that they become better suited to the conditions they live in.

exoskeleton
The hard outer layer of an insect that protects the soft parts inside.

extinction
The total, worldwide dying out of any plant or animal species.

falconry
Flying falcons or hawks as a sport. Also called hawking.

feral
Domestic animals that have escaped or been abandoned and are now living freely in the wild.

fertilization
The joining together of a male sperm and a female egg to start a new life.

filter-feeder
An animal that sieves water through giant combs called gill rakers, for small particles of food.

flehmen
A behaviour shown by many male mammals, where they curl their lips back and smell the air, searching for important odours. Female equids and young also occasionally use the flehman response.

fossil
The remains of a once-living plant or animal that have turned to stone over thousands or millions of years.

fovea
The sensitive area at the back of the eye in birds and primates that enables them to see in sharp detail.

gait
The way an animal moves at certain speeds. It refers to the order in which an animal moves its legs.

gene/genetics
The code for a physical trait and the way this is passed from one generation to another. Each gene contains a strand of DNA that is responsible for a feature, such as blue eyes.

gill
Part of an animal's body used for breathing underwater.

grazer
An animal that feeds on grass, for example a horse or antelope.

groom
The way an animal cares for its coat and skin. It can be carried out by the animal itself or by one animal for another.

habitat
The particular place where a group of animals live, such as a rainforest or a desert.

hemisphere
One half of the Earth, divided by the equator. The northern hemisphere lies above the equator, the southern hemisphere below it.

herbicide
A substance used to kill weeds.

herbivore
An animal that eats only plant food.

herd
A group of particular animals that remain together, such as elephants or wildebeest.

hibernation
A period of sleep during the winter when body processes slow down. Animals, such as bears, hibernate mainly because food is scarce and they might starve otherwise.

incisor teeth
Sharp teeth in the front of a mammal's mouth that are used for biting and nibbling food.

infrasound
Very low sound that cannot be heard by humans although we can sometimes feel the vibrations caused by the sound.

insect
An invertebrate (no backbone) animal which has three body parts, six legs and usually two pairs of wings. Beetles, ants and butterflies are all insects.

insecticide
Any artificially manufactured substance that is used to kill insects.

instinct
An inherited response to a particular stimulus that is common to all those in the same species. This is a response that is not taught to them but is a biological need. Animals use their instincts in hunting and reproduction.

intestine
Part of an animal's gut where food is broken down and absorbed into the body.

joint
The point of contact between two bones, this also includes the ligaments that join them.

keratin
A horny substance that makes up a snake's scales.

larva (plural larvae)
The young of insects that undergo complete metamorphosis, such as beetles, butterflies and true flies. Larvae can be grubs, maggots or caterpillars.

Latin name
The scientific name for a species. An animal often has many different common names. For example, the bird called an osprey in Europe is often referred to as a fish hawk in North America. The Latin name is the same worldwide.

lens
The transparent part of an animal's eye that focuses the light on to the light-sensitive cells at the back of the eye.

liver
An organ that processes food from the digestive system (gut). One of the liver's main tasks is to remove any poisons from the blood.

livestock
Domesticated animals such as sheep, cattle, pigs and poultry that are kept for producing meat, milk and wool or for breeding purposes.

lung
An organ of the body that takes in oxygen from the air.

lyriform organ
A sensory organ, especially on the legs of spiders, that picks up vibrations.

malaria
An infectious disease that is passed to humans and some animals by the bite of a mosquito.

mammal
A warm-blooded animal with a backbone. Most have hair or fur. Mammals feed their offspring on milk from the mother's body.

migration
A regular journey some animals make from one habitat to another, because of changes in the weather or their food supply, or to breed.

minibeasts
Small creatures such as insects, spiders and centipedes.

molar
A broad, ridged tooth in the back of a mammal's jaw, used for grinding up food.

muscle
An animal tissue made up of bundles of cells that can contract (shorten) to produce movement.

native
An animal that originates in a particular place.

nocturnal
An animal that rests by day and is active during the night.

oesophagus
Part of the gut of an animal, usually long and tube-shaped. It transports swallowed food from the mouth to the stomach.

organ
A part of the body or plant that has a special function, for example, a kidney in the body, or a leaf in a plant.

palps
Short stalks that project from the mouthparts of a butterfly, moth or spider and that act as sensors.

paralyse
To make an animal completely powerless and unable to move, even though it is still alive.

parasites
Animals, such as fleas and ticks, that live on other animals and harm them by feeding on them, although they do not usually kill them.

pest
A living thing, such as an insect, that has a damaging effect on other animals or plants.

pesticides
Chemicals that are sprayed on to plants to kill pests, especially insects.

pits
Heat sensors located on either side of a snake's head.

plains
An area of flat land without any hills.

plantation
An area of land that is planted with a certain crop which is sold to make money.

poaching
Capturing and/or killing animals illegally and selling them for commercial gains.

polar region
The area around the North or South Pole, where it is very cold.

pollination
The transfer of pollen from the male part of a flower to the female part, so that the plant can be fertilized and produce seeds.

population
The number of people or animals or plants of the same species that live in a particular area.

predator
An animal that hunts and kills other animals for food.

prehensile tail
A tail that can grasp and hold on to objects such as branches. Monkeys have prehensile tails.

preserve
To keep safe from danger or death.

prey
An animal that is hunted by other animals for food.

pride
A number of lions that keep together as a group.

primates
A group of intelligent mammals that includes lemurs, bush-babies, monkeys, apes and humans. Primates mainly live in trees and have limbs adapted for climbing, swinging or leaping.

rainforest
A tropical forest where it is hot and wet all year round.

raptor
Any bird of prey. From the Latin *rapere* meaning to seize, grasp or take by force.

rare
Animals that only exist in small numbers and are not found often.

receptor
A cell or part of a cell that is designed to respond to a particular stimulus such as light, heat or smell.

regurgitate
To bring up food that has already been swallowed.

reproduction
When a male and female get together to produce offspring.

reptile
A scaly, air-breathing cold-blooded animal with a backbone. This group includes tortoises, snakes and crocodilians.

saliva
A colourless liquid that is produced by glands in the mouth.

salt gland
An organ on a crocodile's tongue that gets rid of excess salt.

scavenger
An animal that feeds on the remains of dead animals.

scent
A smell. For instance, social insects give off scents to communicate a wide range of messages that influence the behaviour within the nest.

sedate
To calm or quieten an animal by giving it a drug known as a sedative.

sense
Any of the five main faculties used by an animal to obtain information: sight, hearing, smell, taste and touch.

sensory system
The collection of organs and cells by which an animal is able to receive messages from its surroundings.

skeleton
The framework of bones that supports and often protects the body of an animal and to which the muscles are usually attached.

slaughter
The killing of animals, especially for food.

smuggling
Taking goods (or animals) into or out of a country illegally.

species
Animals and plants that belong to the same species are all so similar to each other that they can breed together successfully. All species have their own Latin name.

spinneret
An opening that is found at the end of a spider's abdomen. It is through this that silk is pulled out.

spiracles
The holes in the sides of an insect's body through which air passes into breathing tubes.

stimulus
Something such as heat or light that causes a specific physical response in the body.

streamlined
Shaped to slip through air or water easily without much resistance.

subspecies
A wide-ranging species may adapt to local conditions, and look different in some parts of the world. These different forms are called subspecies, but the animals are still able to breed together if they meet.

talon
A hooked claw, especially on a bird of prey.

tapetum
Reflective layer at the back of some animals' eyes that makes them glow when light shines into them.

temperate
Areas of the Earth that have a moderate climate. They are not as hot as the tropics nor as cold as the Arctic and the Antarctic.

termite
An ant-like insect that lives in highly organized colonies, in tropical areas.

territory
An area that an animal uses for feeding or breeding. Some animals defend their territories against others of the same species.

thorax
The middle section of an insect's body. The insect's wings and legs are attached to the thorax.

trachea
The windpipe running from the nose and mouth to transport air to the lungs.

venom
Poisonous fluid produced in the glands of some snakes and by nearly all spiders that is used to kill their prey.

vertebrate
Any animal that has a backbone. For example birds, mammals and reptiles.

warm-blooded
An animal that maintains its body temperature at the same level all the time.

whaling
The hunting of whales for their meat and blubber.

Index

This edition is published by Lorenz Books

Lorenz Books is an imprint of Anness Publishing Ltd
Hermes House, 88–89 Blackfriars Road, London SE1 8HA
tel. 020 7401 2077; fax 020 7633 9499
www.lorenzbooks.com; info@anness.com

© Anness Publishing Ltd 2003, 2005

UK agent: The Manning Partnership Ltd, 6 The Old Dairy, Melcombe Road, Bath BA2 5LR
tel. 01225 478444; fax 01225 478440; sales@manning-partnership.co.uk

UK distributor: Grantham Book Services Ltd, Isaac Newton Way, Alma Park Industrial Estate, Grantham, Lincs NG31 9SD
tel. 01476 541080; fax 01476 541061; orders@gbs.tbs-ltd.co.uk

North American agent/distributor: National Book Network, 4501 Forbes Boulevard, Suite 200, Lanham, MD 20706
tel. 301 459 3366; fax 301 429 5746; www.nbnbooks.com

Australian agent/distributor: Pan Macmillan Australia, Level 18, St Martins Tower, 31 Market St, Sydney, NSW 2000
tel. 1300 135 113; fax 1300 135 103; customer.service@macmillan.com.au

New Zealand agent/distributor: David Bateman Ltd, 30 Tarndale Grove, Off Bush Road, Albany, Auckland
tel. (09) 415 7664; fax (09) 415 8892

Publisher: Joanna Lorenz
Editorial Director: Judith Simons
Editor: Sarah Uttridge
Authors: Michael Bright,
John Farndon, Tom Jackson,
Robin Kerrod, Rhonda Klevansky,
Dr Jen Green, Barbara Taylor
Illustrators: Julian Baker, Peter Bull,
Vanessa Card, Stuart Carter, Linden Artists,
Rob Sheffield, Sarah Smith, David Webb
Designers: Joyce Mason, Alix Wood

Previously published as
Illustrated Wildlife Encyclopedia: Animal Planet

1 3 5 7 9 10 8 6 4 2

PICTURE CREDITS

NOTES

NOTES

NOTES

NOTES

NOTES

NOTES